HOW TO DISCOVER AND IMPROVE YOUR SKILLS

2021 EDITION

Table of Contents

INTRODUCTION

The talent (the τάλαντον Greek, meaning talanton balance or weight) was a unit of monetary measure used in ancient times. He acquired fame for his mention in one of Jesus' parables: the parable of the talents, from whose interpretation "intelligence," "aptitude" derives.

From a human resources perspective, the concept of talent is understood as a whole, where knowledge and attitudes are mixed. Knowledge is acquired and therefore is available to anyone; attitudes are available to anyone who wishes to adopt them.

According to experts, talent is described as the characteristic of those people whose abilities are committed to doing things that improve the results of the organization. In this way, we are faced with a committed professional who puts into practice his abilities to obtain superior results in his environment.

On the other hand, the development and application of talent by professionals is not located in the amount and volume of knowledge, but rather in the ability to learn and transfer the new skills achieving a positive and important impact on our environment organizational. In this ebook, I will give you the tools to develop your talent, right mindset to achieve it. Sit back, pour yourself a glass of drink, and enjoy.

CHAPTER 1: *HOW TO DISCOVER YOUR TALENT*

If you are reading this ebook, it is because you are thinking about how to discover your talent. This process does not have to be easy, although we are not saying it is impossible either.

In this chapter, we will help you to assume certain paradigms that make it easier to find your talent, and we will give you clues so that you can discover it.

We also wanted to support you with other more visual content, so you can take tools and know how to go through this introspective process.

Talent can be discovered

And first, to understand that perceiving our interior requires effort and attention, and sometimes, even with much effort, it is not easy to identify the talent that characterizes us.

Talent can appear after many years and is usually in the least expected place; for example, in our sessions, we work with people who have skills in things that they thought were bad.

Most people don't know what their talent is. Discovering your talents and knowing them well allows you to find your place in the world both socially and professionally, as well as in other vital areas.

Picasso used to say that " inspiration always comes to work" , no study or science has been able to solve the mystery of inspiration, so it is necessary to visualize new realities, remain active listening and let the goddess Fortuna visit you.

" The secret of existence is not only to live but to know what you live for " (Fiódor Dostoievski)

The process is not immediate, we need the effort to achieve this goal, but each of us has a thousand and more reasons to start the path of discovering his own talent, so there is no surrender.

Novalis, an eighteenth-century German poet, was in love with the invisible and came to consider that there was light in the darkness. According to Bill Viola (2011), pioneer artist in the use of new means of expression:

"The known and the unknown are immersed in a continuous dance within us and around us... What our senses reveal to us about the world is only the surface of a much deeper and unknown reality. Science has taught us that most of the cosmos is imperceptible to the reduced bandwidths of energy available to our senses."

In short, don't give up; talent is there. That you have not identified it already or that you feel that you have disengaged from that search does not ensure that you are not able to find it. First, we have to deactivate our autopilot and know where to look, let's go there!

1.1 STEP 1: DISCOVER YOURSELF

The writer José Luis Sampedro, at the Menéndez Pelayo University, on the Summer Courses of 2010, encouraged to "make themselves present, because very few become what they could have been, in this it is where you don't have to save the fight."

The Ability To Know Himself

"Know yourself" is an expression attributed to Socrates, who recommends paying attention to the inner voice, the voice of consciousness, of the soul, knowing oneself is very complex because it is something that is changing all the time.

To know oneself, there must be freedom to look. The Socratic maxim guides us to know our true essence, beyond the superficial layer of beliefs with which we have constructed the disguise of our personality.

However, the word person in Greek means mask, so we need to discover our interior, where the source of well-being and happiness resides, is a process of self-discovery and personal development.

In most cases, having confidence in yourself, a state of energy and joy, mental clarity, inner happiness, faith in yourself and what you have to do is essential for us to develop our talents.

Change As A Way To Find Your Talent

It is never too late to find your vocation, and this can happen at any age and implies a total change in favor of motivation and well-being, talent is what really makes you happy, makes you a unique being.

In short, knowing who you are and understanding that you are the starting point is essential to start discovering your talent.

1.2 STEP 2. BE AWARE OF YOUR SENSATIONS AND EMOTIONS

Krishnamurti (2009), to illustrate the meaning of "be yourself," said: "The seed of oak can never be transformed into a pine."

Every activity you start can take your talent, and discover it is necessary not to close doors in your path, but to pay your attention to more possible elements, and above all listen to your feelings.

Learn To Manage Emotions

To find your talent, it is necessary to start by examining your level of frustration, emptiness or fullness to begin with the search for change; then limit the fear of failure, taking care of your interests, so you will succeed more likely; Then start exploring your strengths.

It is important not to forget that we all need time and patience to discover what our talent is.

In short, listening to your body will help you locate yourself. You are about to undertake a change, and in the face of this search, the body will tend to manifest itself, in the form of frustration, making you think of failures, etc.

1.3 STEP 3: UNDERSTAND WHAT TALENT IS

To define a talent we do not have to think simply of being professional dancers or playing in a rock group, a talent has several shapes, sizes and extends to many areas of life.

For example, you might now ask yourself: am I able to interpret people's emotions? You may not realize it or do not value it very much, but I assure you that this is a very useful talent in the world of social life, in fact, it must be valued and developed.

The List Of The 34 Talents

The Gallup Institute is known for the list of 34 talents, based on studies of millions of people, they have managed to know 34 points that to a greater or lesser extent exist in a person, of all these talents, there will be some in which you will be good , and you can find them.

1. **The worker:** Person who needs to be in constant activity, performing some task.
2. **The activator:** Person who gives rise to things taking action.
3. **The flexible:** Person who adapts to the unforeseen.
4. **The analytical** - Objective: Person who loves the empirical, who acts following the logic.
5. **The organizer, the conductor:** Person who optimizes the result by managing several variables in unison.
6. **The one who follows his personal convictions:** Person who is guided according to his values, through integrity and congruence.
7. **The leader:** Person who assumes the positions, orders, and entrusts them.
8. **The communicator**: Person who encourages the rest through communication, takes care of passing messages, captivatingly.
9. **The competitive:** Person, who focuses on the rest to motivate, is also aware of the level of competence of others.
10. **Feeling part of something broader:** A person who feels united to others, being aware of the importance of globality.
11. **Past / Person who takes the past as a reference:** Person who addresses a situation using the past, getting to understand it, and managing to reach a solution.
12. **The prudent**: Person, who checks, watches the rest, knowing in the place you must put your feet and the rest.
13. **The potential discoverer:** Person who reveals the talent of the rest, and who is responsible for supporting them.
14. **The disciplinary:** Person who establishes predictability, structuring the world through detail and specificity.
15. **The empathetic** Person who maintains the ability to put himself in the place of another person, coming to feel what that person feels.
16. **The fair.** The person who follows the path of equality, trying to make fair decisions.

17. **The focuser** Person who focuses on the decision previously made and does not abandon it until he has achieved its objective.
18. **The futuristic / visionary.** The person who detects what will happen before the others. With great ability to view the future.
19. **The harmonic** Person who is responsible for generating harmony among the people around him.
20. **The creative** Person who generates ideas, approaching the world from other perspectives with creativity.
21. **Who integrates:** Person who is dedicated to including people in a group, and that they feel welcomed generating in them a feeling of belonging.
22. **The one that takes care of the individualization:** Person that detects the special qualities of each person, and makes it act in function of these.
23. **The "Input" - Information input:** Person who expands information, collects, and documents.
24. **The intellectual:** Person who likes to deepen, characterized by the taste towards intellectualization.
25. **The apprentice**: Person thirsty to learn. For these people, learning is a pleasure.
26. **The optimizer:** Person who seeks to extract the best of situations. Making it work better than it did before.
27. **Who repairs:** Person who repairs the breakage of a situation, making a diagnosis and subsequent repair.
28. **The positive:** Enthusiastic person, which, through that attitude, manages to infect others.
29. **The relational:** Person who feeds and tries to maintain the relationship, trying to generate a high level of trust and fidelity.
30. **The responsible;** Person committed to carrying out what he says, with honesty and loyalty.
31. **The confident;** Person who turns criticism into constructive, convinced to move forward, sure of herself and her abilities.
32. **The original / different:** Person who likes to stand out and distinguish himself from the rest. He also likes to be heard and admired.
33. **The strategist:** Person who is able to anticipate and choose the best starting approaches.
34. **Power of conviction:** Person with the talent to convince and seduce others, coming to unite them for the same cause.

In short, to know how to find your talent you first have to understand what talent is and secondly have a broad lexicon that allows you to more easily locate what your talents are or those characteristics that ultimately define you.

What Is The Secret To Discover The Talent?

In order to be considered talent, the presence of a particular element, passion, is necessary. This allows you to identify talent and differentiate it from any other activity.

Feeling passion while doing an activity leads you to consider what you do as a pleasure and not an obligation. From there, a circle is generated where passion leads you to discover a talent for a certain activity, and this leads you to always feel more passion when you do it.

Ask yourself:

- Really, what am I good at? What do I consider my best qualities? What would I like to do during my life, where would I work? What would I like to learn more than anything in the world?
- It can be anything, from what you wanted to be as a child, from mastering applications to flirt online, to something you never expected.
- When Jules Verne discovers with his imagination to be able to go around the earth, he is visualizing a new reality, using parameters other than those known. No one doubts that this was one of his talents.

1.4 STEP 4: KEYS TO DISCOVER YOUR TALENT

Key 1. Is Talent Something Past Or Future?

There are talents that you will discover in the future, but the search for a talent you already have, you have to start looking back, reflect on your experiences.

Summarizing. What you have achieved, what has made you proud of yourself, are signs that speak of episodes where we can find our talent; Of course, childhood is the place where our first skills live.

Exercise to find your talent write the story of your life in 10 or 15 pages. This exercise will help you discover the talents you have and those that you have to develop more.

Write about what type of child you were, what you liked to do before and after homework, about how you grew up, about your place of life, and then write your future, about the places you want to visit, what things you want to get, etc.

Summarizing. This exercise will help you to know your priorities, what you really consider important about yourself, what you want in life. It will also help you to know the talents that you must cultivate, thus being able to achieve your real goals.

Key 2. Talent In The Difficulties

In addition to childhood, also the episodes of life's challenges are important to discover a talent, overcoming complex situations leaves you more satisfied with yourself, because, maybe, before this situation, you didn't know you could achieve the goal you had what to face.

In the test moments, when you leave your comfortable and familiar environment, it is when you learn more about yourself, if you close yourself to the challenges by resigning yourself to a quiet life, if you go back when the moments become difficult, or you run away from problems, you will deny the opportunity to excel.

In short, our experiences also talk about us, about the capabilities we have put in place. Do not underestimate the sacrifices or challenge we have been through. Although society tells us that it is usual to be resilient and that for this, we must know how to face adversity, leaving them strengthened. They also give us information about who we are.

Key 3. Body Signals

- ***Sensations***

The activities that leave you with a pleasant feeling are an alarm that your body uses to indicate that what you are doing you really like.

These activities nourish your brain and your interior, that is, the things that make you happy also reveal your talents. Reflect on those activities in which you enjoy. They can be a suitable guide to find talent, your talent.

- ***Time Awareness***

Think also if when you are involved in a certain activity, you lose consciousness of the time that passes. Mihály Csíkszentmihályi talked about the state of flow referring to this state.

- ***Listen***

Listen to the way you talk about something, for example, if you've ever talked non-stop to a family member or best friend about a certain topic that is very important to you, this may be another clue to a talent.

Key 4. Environment Signals

Life leaves you little demonstrations through experiences of what your talent can be:

- ***Observe Your Group***

Think about whether others congratulate you for what you do, or if they ask for your help in doing so, you may think that it is not a talent, but it is likely that it is. If you help others, you will see another perspective, and you can discover some talent that you did not know you had or develop new talent with this exercise.

Discovering talent is trying to connect people with the best of themselves, and discover the potential that each of us holds within themselves.

- **What Is Easy For You**

Evaluate what you are good at, sometimes your talents are the things you love to do, but it is important to remember that our talents are usually things that we do not have the consciousness that we enjoy or that we do not even think about.

That is why it is important to thoroughly evaluate what we are good at. Think of what is natural to you, things that don't cost you hardly any effort. Sometimes, for example, there are people who correct others, this behavior usually indicates something in which the person is good and in which he knows in depth.

- **Successful Episodes**

Think about the episodes in which you have succeeded, such as helping a friend organize his house. By the way, the organization is a very useful talent.

- **Travels**

Travel to expand your experiences. Facing new contexts and challenges will teach you more about yourself than you thought you could do or not do.

Key 5. How Do You Manage Your Time?

Your time is very important, dedicating the time you have available to new activities can help you discover the talent you did not know if you spend all day on the couch after work you will have very little time to discover yourself.

Your talents are in activities that you have not yet tried and in which you will have the possibility to go beyond what you are now.

The reality seen from the perception of the five senses is very limited, our life is full of beliefs, some are empowering, and others were limiting. The first move towards change is focused on our growth and open the way to get where we want. The second, limiting beliefs restrict us and become obstacles, preventing us from moving forward.

How you dedicate your time on the day is also essential. Think about what your priorities are and try to find ways to have more time so you can experience new things.

If there is an activity that interests you and you want to develop, consider taking classes, get more information will tell you if it can really be a talent of yours.

Give yourself time, self-discovery demands a lot of self-reflection and spending part of your time with yourself serves to understand you better.

In short, let's try to be aware of our time. Try not to victimize or blame yourself for the time you have or how you are investing it. Both postures make you stay passive, and there are no changes. Encourage yourself to take responsibility for owning it; that is your ally to find your talent.

Key 6. You Don't Know, But You Have A Treasure, Value It!

Develop the skills you already have. Take advantage of the engine that is taking you to read this section and introduce changes.

It is likely that you have some basic skills; each of these can become your talent. To discover it, it will take a lot of commitment to get into several activities so that this talent comes to light because perhaps you have experienced only a minimal aspect of some potential talent.

It's complicated that we know what our talents are and gifts if we never ask for them. We go through life without stopping to think about what we are good at, what we like or what we dream of doing in the future, and that makes it difficult to discover and enjoy your talent or talents.

This inability can be born of a lack of self-confidence. We leave you another video on how to improve your confidence, to make it easier for you to value yourself, and thus locate that treasure that seems to be within you.

Step 5: Learn About The Talent Concept

There are talents and gifts as people exist in the world; each one has something special. Let's put light on the concept of talent.

An aid to discover talent is to know the various talents that exist and that we have already incorporated as a base, a classification can be very useful because each type of talent is hidden in a different way, and requires a different way to find it.

Ways You Can Have The Talent

Before we have exposed you a list with the 34 talents that are identified. Now we are going to explain the groupings that talents can have. To better understand the concept of talent.

The obvious talent: it is easy to detect; it is a skill that you already have by nature, and no effort is needed to see it.

The hidden talent: it is the talent we have, but you don't find out about this, sometimes because you think it's so normal that you don't see it as something special of your own or because you think everyone has it.

As with obvious talent, hidden talent is also a skill that you already have by nature and no effort is needed to grow

The potential talent: it is the talent that you think you do not have and that you want, and the mere fact of wishing something so much, is the fundamental tool to develop this potential that can become the best talent you will have.

Potential talent is a part of you that however you have to exercise a lot, all this desire can push you to make an effort to work it, and this effort can make it develop a lot, although, if we do not do it there is a risk that it I fell asleep forever.

Summarizing, to know what we have to look for, we have to be clear about where to look, and for this it is not only necessary that you know all the talents that can be had and / or developed but also understand what talent is and the various forms that can have : Obvious, hidden and potential.

Step 6: Act

Many people expect the day, the moment, the circumstance, the right situation to arrive, but in reality today, this very moment is a gift that you have and perhaps you have not valued properly.

Beat Your Fears

Everyone is interested in something, and many possibilities are in this world to be discovered.

Putting aside doubts and thinking about what makes you happy and you do n't have a hard time doing, is a strategy to discover what your true talents and abilities are, but if you understand that you have a talent and that your studies or profession are not related to That talent, this can generate fear.

On the other hand, if you decide to fight and strengthen your talent, you may have to give up many things, and fear kills dreams, but if you find what you are passionate about, you will never think about retiring or arriving on Friday afternoon or holidays.

When you know what you were born for, what talent you have and can use, is when the "how to do that" loses importance.

As we have just seen, something that can make you not act is fear. This paralyzes us, slows us down.

In short, talent could say that it is an antagonist of fear. Fear makes us paralyze, and talent loves movement. We understand then that to identify our talent, and it will be essential to act.

Step 7. Where To Look For The Talent

Surely, there are unexplored dimensions of your life, or that you have explored but not enough.

3 Places Where To Find Your Talent

1. One is the one that has to do with your natural gifts, personal traits, in what you are good at.
2. Another is the one that has to do with your experience because the undeveloped talent is of no use
3. *Another is that which has to do with passion, to develop and live from a talent it is necessary to record, and if your reasons are not based on your personal interests, you will end up getting tired.*

What attitude are you having?

An example of an attitude that you can translate into talent is: «I love to talk, I would be talking for hours and hours. Have you tried to be a lecturer, to be an announcer on a radio, to be a teacher?

CG Jung , an American psychologist, says: " Man believes that he shapes those ideas, but in reality, it is they who mold him and make him his unconscious interpreter ... We do not create them, and they create us ."

Man is only the server of his ideas that tries to shape them, in the creative process, according to the author, there are two times: what the creative awakening produces in man, through the impact on the consciousness of ideas that emanate from some superior source, and the minor ideas, visions, and concepts that he captures and shapes.

Only the power of the mind can change the impossible into possible, transforming the "I can't" into "I can."

" Just as there is an atmosphere created by the oxygen of plants, there is a noosphere (sphere of ideas) created by the collective unconscious " Gerardo Pereiro (2007).

Is Talent Innate Or Acquired?

Talent can be innate or acquired, and there are many ways to discover it. For example:

- Remember the activities of the school and think about which one you stood out.
- Discover the balance between challenge and skill, to perform the activity to your needs with the same enthusiasm from start to finish.
- Take the right time to practice (according to the University of Pennsylvania), the more you reinforce your talent, the better you will perform.

In short, it is important to know where to look and understand if it is innate or acquired.

1.5 STEP 8. KNOW WHY I AM NOT FINDING MY TALENT

Causes Why You Are Not Found Your Talent

"I think I don't have any talent or passion," "I need to focus, I don't know myself or know what my gift is in this life," "How can I know my talent? I have nothing clear, "I do not know what to do with my life. I am lost in my work and do not know where to go. "

First Cause: Having limiting beliefs

The reason why you have not yet discovered your talents, is because you have been surrounded by a system that has not allowed you to detect it, so, if you do not know your talent, do not blame yourself , your education in all probability did not allow you to explore adequately the possibilities offered (and still offering) life.

The problem is, as it happened to the majority in your youth, to believe that what those who "knew more than us" told you must be true. That way, you limited your options to discover your natural talents.

Social beliefs have prevented you from developing your full potential, phrases like "music or art do not feed" have been repeated to the full by parents and guardians, but, perhaps some of us do not appreciate the music created of course by the musicians?

Probably you could only have access to the training and education that your parents and educational centers provided you, the need to succeed through established and standardized canons made you leave aside those things that you were best given to dedicate yourself to others that supposedly they would bring success to your life, so you lost the source that fed your talents, that is creativity.

In short, don't judge yourself or blame yourself for not yet finding your talent. Society often does not make it easy.

Second Cause: You Are Wanted Only In The Context

Trying to find your talent in the educational system we have, means limiting your possibilities and even expectations.

The education we have can give us indications of whether we are good in science or literature, but it is very likely that our talent goes from being perceived in school, and when your talent is not within a profession standardized by society and is something different, something new, people will not believe that this is possible, and neither will you.

In short, it may be that the context has not made it easy for you to understand what you are good at and that as a consequence you have been able to build your life in that direction. But circumstances are not what makes us slaves, but how we react to them. We must be responsible for finding ourselves in contexts that favor us.

Third Cause: Not Understanding the Differences Between Talent and Adaptation

The difference is that, when you talk about your true talent, passion makes your eyes shine with your own light; This question pushes us to think of people who have been exceptionally talented (Leonardo Da Vinci, Einstein, etc.).

Many times talent is associated with the ability to do something in an outstanding way, so it is difficult for a normal person to compare, but in reality, we all have a talent, whatever the measure, but we have it, what happens is that We make it invisible because the response that people want to hear is preferred.

At the time in which we live the "normal" jobs do not exist, and now everyone must develop their latent potential inside, the external pressure for the situation in which we are in crisis should give us enough strength to look at our inside.

In short, in order to really discover what your passion is, you need a work of personal development. So you can have the clear ideas of what you really want for your future, without falling into false illusions, not guiding you by what others can tell you, but by guiding you by your intuition, for what you really love and what you enjoy doing.

What If I Still Without Finding My Talent?

Believing that you don't have any talent, just means creating a protection zone, a comfort zone, but you have to leave this area.

This is what happens with a hidden talent, but those talents are not lost, they are simply buried waiting for you to bring them to light, all you have to do, like when you look for anything else, is to explore the place Right, talent is an inseparable part of you, so it is within you, and that's where you have to look.

There are people who do not shine their talents for fear of insulting or dulling others, but as Mary Ann Williamson said:

"Our deepest fear is not that we are inadequate; Our deepest fear is that we are even more powerful than we imagine. It is our light, not our darkness that scares us the most.

While we free ourselves from our fears (to make our light shine with our talents), our presence frees others. "

Horace Walpole, British writer, and architect, who wrote in 1754 Serendipity, the story of the three princesses of "Serendip," a traditional Persian story full of amazing qualities, the princesses had the happy ability to make unexpected discoveries of things they did not seek, while they looked for other things.

1.6 STEP 8: KNOW THE TECHNIQUES TO FIND YOUR TALENT

Creativity. An Alliance Of Talent

"There is no doubt that creativity is the most important human resource of all. Without creativity, there would be no progress, and we would be constantly repeating the same patterns" Edward de Bono.

The creative product always carries a transformation, as towards Neruda, when it combines words in a new way to obtain an unknown poetic image, or as Kandinsky did to achieve a new pictorial language.

Creativity is an abstract concept, and, consequently, it is difficult to develop this ability. Not all of us are creative by nature, but we can all develop our creativity to find different solutions.

" I am not a painter, nor a musician, but I am creative " Osho.

We have the ability to choose, we cannot be spectators of life, but creators, and you must be the driver of your life.

To become creative, you have to establish new beliefs, think "I am creative," because as you think you are. Every creative process is unconscious, oblivious to reason, and uncontrollable.

Creative ideas flow when we are able to trust our interior, our own instincts because many times, we do not listen to them because of fears or blockages, whether emotional, cultural, educational or social.

We can never know what is the unknown, because at the time recognized as the unknown, has returned to the known, the recognition process is a process in which the known continues. Since I don't know what the unknown is, I can only do one thing: eliminate thinking as it emerges.

Creativity Techniques to Find and Develop Talent

"It is what I have unknown in myself that makes me" Paul Valéry (French poet of the twentieth century).

Creativity techniques are methods that serve to stimulate in a creative sense, including techniques for generating ideas and to stimulate divergent thinking or problem rethinking methods.

Do It

Robert W. Olsen's method, is a structured process of creativity, in which you have to do an essential preliminary work that helps you extract the best of creative tools; Do it is the acronym for: define the problem (d), open mind, that is, open mind and application of creative techniques (o), identify the best solution (i) and transform (t).

Scamper Method

The "Scamper Method" is a technique to promote creativity and creative thinking developed by Bob Eberlee in the 20s, the technique consists of a very detailed checklist where you can generate new ideas when you start working with a basic idea.

Method 3-6-5

"Method 3-6-5" is a technique in which you have to write some ideas on paper and pass it on to your friends, they will receive your ideas, write additional ideas and pass them on to the next participant, to generate many different ideas.

Mental Map

The "Mind Map" is a diagram used to represent ideas, words, tasks and other related concepts that revolve around an idea or a keyword, to synthesize information and a logical and creative way of expressing ideas.

Maslow, when investigating the creative attitude, observed that the creative person, in the phase of inspiration, loses his past and his future and lives only the moment; It is like entering a mystical experience, this ability to "get lost in the present" is a sign of any creative process.

In short, talent can be developed. And here we wanted to leave you some techniques to help you in this process.

The Analysis Of Personal Purpose. Another Technique To Develop Your Talent

There is the method of psychologist Iván Pirogóv, called the analysis of personal purpose:

- "The first thing you should do is remember all your dreams: what did you dream of in your childhood, in your adolescence, in school, in college, in adult life.
- Now is the time to divide your dreams into two groups, "have" and "be," the dreams of the "have" group are those that are related to owning something, the dreams of the "being" group are those where you see yourself in Some paper, doing something, writes the category "be" in a separate column.
- Think about whether you felt any special emotions when observing people of a certain profession and if you would like to be in their place.
- Add the activities that give you pleasure.
- Now check if all the targeted dreams cause you some internal emotional response, to do so, visualize each point on the "be" list and listen carefully to the emotions and feelings that it causes you. What do you feel while doing it?
- Then rate your strength on a scale of 0 to 10.
- Discard the dreams that obtained the lowest scores in the previous step.
- Now you have a real list of your innate tendencies formulated as dreams, but what points on the list could you group?
- Look at the grouped points of the list and give each group a name.

- It is necessary to understand how the groups are related, and the groups usually have links of mutual support.
- Now write down all the possible options of how you could apply your talents in real life.
- Rate each item on the list on a scale of 0 to 10. 10, a very desirable option; 0, the least acceptable option.
- Then, define a specific direction; this profession will bring you success, joy in life."

What Does The Science Of Talent Say?: Talent Under Physical Perspective

The Infant Education Congress at the Palace of Congresses and Exhibitions in Madrid (2010), is inspired by the principles of quantum physics:

"Creativity does not arise by chance, it needs the favorable conditions for creative ideas to flow, it is a process that begins by preparing and plowing the earth, following the simile of Paulo Coelho, followed by careful planting that must be nurtured and expected until ripeness arrives, an epiphany of absolute lucidity, to end the harvest, time to collect the final fruit".

The creative process is not linear or exclusive; It is recurrent, and several phases can be superimposed at the same time. Being creative is inherent to the human being, Amit Goswami (2009) physics researcher explains:

"As we grow, we are creative in our quantum self-identity, constantly discovering new contexts of life, of human essence. When we discover a new context, we also explore the secondary contexts that exist at our disposal by combining the new contexts with the learned contexts (we adapt and integrate); This is a stage of homeostatic adaptation. "

All creativity is based on "quantum leaps": of something that did not exist before because it belonged to the unknown world, suddenly, it begins to have life and becomes part of our conscious world, when there is an intention to transcend the everyday, You must learn to think, dream and imagine with other parameters, from a quantum point of view, creative ideas must be sought in the virtual realm, in the uncircumcised mind, in the universal spirit, where everything is potential.

"The repressed feelings are relegated to the unconscious and generate blockages in the flow of vital energy" according to the opinion of Amit Goswami (2009), a prestigious quantum physicist.

People have different ways of expressing their creativity, and each one is creative in its own way, it is unique, unrepeatable and irreplaceable, the dignity of the human being is in its uniqueness and should not be compared with anyone, each individual has been born with a certain gift or talent that is part of your internal chemistry, your physiology, your being.

Know the power of your quantum field" a revealing fact, the result of an investigation conducted at the University of California de los Angeles (UCLA): "97 percent of the children think of in an original way, however at the age of 30 there are only 3 percent of people who do it ".

In the phase of creative inspiration, "Unconscious processing generates a multitude of possibilities, while inspiration is the collapse of one of those possibilities."

As you can see, it is possible to find your talent. In fact, it is necessary, since it is what allows us to differentiate ourselves from the rest. Understanding who we are, what defines us, that we are good at it is essential to be able to build our lives. To be able to feel coherent because each movement we make will be aligned with our talent.

Knowing our potential does not make us unique, but if we cannot find what differentiates us, we can feel empty and dissatisfied.

We hope we have helped you, and we would like you to contribute any opinions you have about it. That you ask any questions, that you seek help if you think you need it.

And for all this we will be willing to listen to you, to understand you and to accompany you in this process of searching for your talent, which can be very rewarding.

resolve a (problem)
for so long that there is n
talent a natu
to do something well: the b
a person or people with
with the ability to be a

CHAPTER 2: *HOW TO GET YOU THE LIFE WITHOUT RESOURCES HAVE YOU THOUGHT TO TAKE?*

You are probably not the only person who, when you wake up and look in the mirror, wonders what reasons you have to go to work, especially if it is a job that does not give you anything and that only obeys the interests of others.

It definitely happened to me.

The next question is whether we are prepared to leave that work that bores us and consumes our energies. If your answer is yes, I congratulate you, and you are in the club of potential entrepreneurs willing to realize the idea they have inside, their idea and their illusion, and make it their life purpose.

Here I will tell you the first steps you will have to take before deciding to undertake.

Before making the decision to leave your job "safe" you should know what the adventure of entrepreneurship is about and first be clear about what you are going to face and then validate if your ideas will be well received in the real world, that is to say if Someone values them and is willing to pay for what you are going to offer.

1. Are you ready to undertake?

First, ask yourself if this adventure is made for you. Like everything in life, leaving the security of a job to launch you to undertake has its advantages and disadvantages. Normally we only know success stories, but as you will imagine behind each of them, there are many frustrating attempts.

To survive this trial-error process, you will need a lot of stamina, patience, and tolerance for frustration. Since starting such a project is not just a career choice, it is also a way of life, and you must ask yourself why you want to do it.

Because if your main reason is to make money fast, it may not be too good for you and you end up getting frustrated sooner than you expect.

We are going to focus for now on the three main reasons to undertake your own project:

1. You are obsessed with solving a certain problem. You have it in your head for a long time, and you will not stop until you achieve it. Being passionate about your idea, that solution to a problem, why, is essential to motivate you during the process that awaits you.
2. You know better than anyone a specific market, or how to solve a specific problem or social need. That particular skill is what will differentiate you from others, from the competition and help you survive.
3. You have always wanted to change the world. This is your opportunity to do it if you are going to undertake it, do it with a purpose and do it in a big way.

- And now ask yourself the following questions:
- Why do I want to undertake?

- What is a success for me?
- How can I imagine changing my life, and how will I impact that of others?
- How do I tolerate frustration and failure?
- What is a commitment to me?

If you have not been able to respond clearly, try again until you identify when you are.

2. Identify your talent

Your talent consists of your strengths and abilities, which you are good at naturally; all this must be the origin of your idea and future business. Without those strengths on your side, you will run out too soon.

What are you good at doing?

Take time to think about what your best skills are in order to direct your effort in that direction.

What skills have helped you so far to get where you are in your life?

How can you improve those skills, refine and refine them to take advantage of them in your entrepreneurial project?

What are your weaknesses? Think about what you could improve and get a sincerity self-assessment as only you know how to do it.

What is your favorite thing to do?

After being clear about what you are good at doing, let's identify what interests you most and excites you in your life:

- What do you most like to do that never bores you and that you wouldn't mind doing it as if it were a job?
- If you could choose what to do with your life regardless of money, what would you do? Do you think you can turn that activity into a business?
- What do you imagine doing in 5 or 10 years?
- What motivates you the most?

Some more qualities that will help you undertake

Logically not everyone starts from the same point. It will also depend on your past, your training, and a series of qualities that will make a difference when undertaking:

A good professional experience related to the idea you want to undertake.

Have decisive intelligence, that is, that ability to see situations in all their magnitude and have the necessary instinct to make the best decisions in the face of problems that arise.

Opening of mind, fundamental to see creative solutions to the most unlikely situations, without prejudice or complex.

Kindness, the key to deal with teams and several interlocutors in unpredictable situations. Never lose your smile and good manners when interacting with others.

3. Define your idea

Before deciding on what your project will be, think of many ideas, the more, the better, and do not become obsessed with one of them, it will probably end up changing and evolving. So do not limit yourself at the beginning, let your creativity flow by pointing everything out without discarding anything.

Deciding on a specific idea will represent giving up on others, do it with reasonable, objective criteria, and before defining yourself for your finalist idea, you should ask yourself the following questions:

- Would people be interested in this idea?
- Do I think this idea could positively impact the lives of others?
- Can my skills offer solutions to people's common problems?
- Remember that the best entrepreneurship ideas usually fulfill these three characteristics:

1- They are simple: they solve a specific problem for a specific type of client.

2- They have a clear benefit: even if it is a single product or service as the main source of income.

3. They focus on a broad market, at least several million potential customers or users.

Therefore, taking into account all of the above, if you are already stuck with an idea, reconsider if that project really suits you and convinces you.

And yet, if your idea does not get out of your mind and does not stop growing in options and possibilities, you may have discovered an extraordinary business potential.

4. Validate your idea

Once you have selected and defined your idea, you will have to research and learn even more about it to understand if it is workable and can work as a project and business.

To validate your idea:

1. Search and study as much as you can about that topic, books, blogs, and publications.
2. Sign up for all events where you can interact with entrepreneurs like you who are developing similar ideas or projects. There you can meet who can advise and guide you.
3. Investigate financing options, costs, and legal options.
4. Analyze the market you are going to face and study your potential competitors.

Do not forget that nobody is going to steal your idea, because an idea is useless, and it has to have a background, an emotion, and knowledge. The best thing you can do is share it and tell it to others, without fear, so that they give you their opinion, a fresh and neutral point of view of someone who is not with the passion of having created something of their own. That feedback from others is the most important part of this trial-error process.

This would be the basic plan to validate your idea:

1- Study your market and the competition you will face.

2- Create your story, a type of speech that you can repeat repeatedly about your idea. Well-structured and trained, so you do not hesitate or wander when someone asks you what it is.

3- Look for cases of failures related to initiatives similar to your idea. It is the best way to understand what they failed and what you don't have to do.

4- Attend events related to your theme, only there will you coincide with the best ones, those that can inspire you and those that you can emulate.

5- Find some of those who would be potential real customers who would be willing to use your product or service, know them and interact with them and find out their reaction to these three key questions:

- Do you understand at first what your idea is about?
- Does it really solve a problem?
- Would you be willing to pay for it?

Do you think that after this review you are ready or ready to undertake? This is the key question that you should be able to answer after this process. Depending on whether your answer is Yes or No, you will have to rethink the next steps to take, redefine and validate your idea, or start the path to launch it.

What you need to transform your idea into a startup

We all have an idea, or several, ideas that come to us at any time, ideas that we have been maturing for a long time. Sometimes we remember them, sometimes we let them pass, and sometimes we point them out. The truth is that it is inevitable that they turn us in the head until we decide to take the first step, that first step that costs so much in the way of shaping them and turning them into a serious project, a startup or a traditional business.

Before considering the way forward to make these ideas a reality, you must ask yourself if that idea fits your life purpose. That purpose that makes you wake up every morning and motivates you in what you do.

Because when you add value to others, if you work your idea and your project thinking about others, you will probably end up doing well, economically, and professionally.

The key is your why what is your purpose?

Most of the time, people do not buy what you do, but the reason why you do it, and that is your purpose, the reason why you do what you do. And that can be applied to personal projects, teams, or large organizations, and if you are not clear about your motivation and there is no purpose behind what you do, you will inevitably end up demotivated.

If you focus your energy on purpose, in addition to realizing what you propose, you will also gain in the long term.

Companies with a purpose, be it a startup, an isolated project, or a succession of projects, will generate more talent and more motivation in you and those around you.

If I am talking more about startups than a traditional company, it is because from now on you are more likely to end up undertaking your idea, alone or with friends, than to continue working in a traditional organization with a pyramid structure, based on the order and command and plunged into the monotony of a position that brings you nothing but the salary at the end of the month.

By definition, a startup is a new, innovative company that will grow under uncertain and changing circumstances. It may or may not be digital, and it may be a platform, an app or another type of business designed to survive in the new VUCA world (Volatile, Uncertain, Complex and Ambiguous). Therefore, new companies, organizations, or startups need leaders and creative entrepreneurs, innovative and growth minded.

The first thing to ask is if your business idea is aligned with your life purpose, your reason for existing, why you would like to be remembered when you are gone. And your idea must be destined not only to fulfill your purpose and be profitable but also to be useful to others.

To do this, try to find the link between these four vital areas:

1. What you like to do the most.
2. What you are good at.
3. For what they could pay you to do.
4. What the world needs.

Well, the point at which these four areas converge is what the Japanese call Ikigai, which becomes your reason for being, the meaning of your life. It is the concept of you must internalize as the reason for your existence that many times you struggle to find it and simply do not achieve it because you are moving in the opposite direction to your interests.

We all have our Ikigai, but to reach it we need deep self-knowledge, so after knowing each other better we can find our purpose.

The concept of Ikigai can also be applied to ideas and entrepreneurship. As you connect these four areas, you will define the direction to give your business idea, something you like, that you are good at doing, that the world needs and for what they are willing to pay you. Therefore, to undertake your idea, it is important that you fit these four areas with your motivation. The motivation and decision you will need to undertake with a purpose are associated with a change of mentality, and that change of mentality goes through these 8 fronts:

1- Choose your purpose and turn it into your idea, your life project.

2 - Reflect on that idea, everything that comes to mind, point it out, mature it, give it as many laps as you need.

3- Spend time, from now on it will be part of your daily life, always give it a space in your agenda.

4 - Prioritize that idea in your day to day, do not just leave it for when you can, or it occurs to you. Force yourself to give it the prominence it deserves. Do not forget that it is your real purpose.

5- Start now, today, not within a month or next year. The ideal conditions to start are never going to happen, and your excuses to postpone and procrastinate can be endless. It is very important that you surround yourself with everything you need so that the lack of means is not an excuse for you either.

6- Get excited. That passion will feed you with energy and motivation. Enjoy that extraordinary feeling and strength.

7- Have discipline, transform the routine of dedicating time to your idea into a habit. Prioritize it over other activities. Lack of time is never a valid argument for someone who sets a goal.

8- Turn that habit into your philosophy of life. It's about living that experience and enjoying it. It's not about being overwhelmed or feeling guilty if you don't make enough progress.

Do you already have an idea in your head?

Many times we find ourselves so involved in our day-to-day lives that routine blocks our good ideas, and our more creative facet is going to be paid. It's normal, don't worry. The positive part is that we have a lot of stimuli around us that allow us to continually refresh our feelings to generate new ideas.

And of all those ideas you will have to select the one that best fits your Ikigai, that is, those that you like, those that you are good at doing, those that you could pay to do and those that the world needs.

Are you ready to come up?

Let's start with what you like.

We all have a passion or even several passions. They can occur in any way, distractions, amusements, hobbies, virtues, or hidden talents. Make a list of everything you have fun doing, by categories, something like:

- Food
- Travel
- Watch movies
- Do sport
- Listen to music
- To design
- Read
- Take a walk
- Talk
- Sound

No matter if it is a list of only one thing or several, the important thing is to have something to keep moving forward and deepening that idea you want to find. The more you advance, the more likely you are to find your idea for that project you could undertake.

In my specific case and to serve as an example, I like to travel. Traveling stimulates me a lot, refreshes my emotions, gives me new perspectives on life, makes me more tolerant and empathic with others, helps me better understand the needs of the societies I visit. Let's start with the concept of traveling:

- Travels
- Nationals
- International
- Urban
- Nature
- Adventure sports
- Cultural
- In a group
- Custom

Let's continue to delve into what interests me, let's choose that I like international travel, both urban and cultural and nature, and that I am preferably looking for experiences with locals that teach me secrets of each place that only they know and that I would never find through a travel agency that offers me plane and hotel packages.

Now let's find solutions to that challenge that I have identified. Some solutions could be:

- **Solution 1:** a social application where you form groups with your friends and offer your travel experience to people who want to join.
- **Solution 2:** an adventure travel agency in which you offer experiences that traditional agencies don't offer
- **Solution 3:** a platform on which you offer alternative experience packages and launch marketing campaigns into the niche of those looking for something like that.
- **Solution 4:** an academy that trains adventurers to transform their passion into a business so that they can earn money by offering their experiences.

After thinking of many solutions like these, this idea has come to me, something like a platform or application that connects adventurous users who are looking for alternative travel experiences with users who are willing to share the experiences they know and on the way to earn money.

Simple no? Well, that would be my solution to the problem. This platform would put them in contact, and their business model would be the commissions for the transactions of those services of experiences through this platform.

CHAPTER 3: *MARKET ANALYSIS*

A market analysis provides you with information about industries, customers, competitors, and other sizes of a market. You can also determine the relationship between supply and demand for a particular product or service. Based on these findings, you make more informed decisions about possible marketing strategies.

What is a market analysis?

How suitable is a particular market for your offer? A market analysis answers this important question. Every market participant, whether a company, founder, or private customer, can conduct a market analysis. In any case, it serves as a basis for decision-making. Suppliers and consumers collect and evaluate information to make buying or selling decisions. You can also rate your current market or look at new markets.

Market analysis is a part of market research and an important part of a business plan . In this, business founders document their business idea in writing. The market analysis systematically examines a given market. The results obtained will allow companies to identify the opportunities and risks of a market. The target group definition forms the basis for market analysis.

Various methods of market analysis

To conduct a market analysis, you need well-founded information. As a rule, small businesses carry out the necessary investigations themselves for their market analysis. By contrast, larger companies often commission market research institutes. A market analysis can be carried out using different methods of data collection. Here a distinction is made between primary research and secondary research.

In the primary research, experts from a target market are interviewed to collect new data. The advantage here: The focus is on the own examination purpose. This allows you to specifically collect the data you need for your market analysis. In contrast, uses secondary research back on existing records from previous studies. These may have been collected both internally and externally. If you opt for the secondary research, you can save both time and money, because you refrain from performing elaborate interviews and their subsequent evaluation. Sources of representative data are, e.g., B. the Federal Statistical Office, professional chambers, annual reports of other companies or journals.

Tip

The bigger your company is, the more comprehensive your market analysis should be.

3.1 Market analysis vs. Market research: Where are the differences?

Market research means the systematic investigation of a particular market. As such, research provides information that enables you to choose a suitable marketing tool. In contrast to market research, the market analysis focuses on the time-related analysis of a specific market. The aim of the market analysis is to identify the most important characteristics of a market and to determine the market structure at a certain point in time.

The market structure designates the structure of a specific market. It results from the interaction of providers and buyers and can be determined by different criteria. These criteria are different characteristics of a market. These include the size and the value as well as the number of providers, the buying behavior of the consumers or even growth forecasts.

What is a market analysis for?

If you want to be successful with your business idea, the preparation of a market analysis is essential. Because a sound market analysis forms the basis for the development of a marketing strategy and concrete marketing measures.

Further reasons why a market analysis pays off for you:

- With market analysis, you can prove your business idea with numbers, data, and facts and convince in the business plan.
- You can identify market potential early on and avoid wrong decisions.
- They recognize any existing knowledge gaps and can close them in good time.
- Market analysis shows you which competitor products are already on the market.
- With market analysis, you can identify the market entry barrier and assess market attractiveness.

Market analysis: content and structure

A meaningful market analysis goes hand in hand with a precise description of the target group and thorough market research. It conveys a holistic picture of a specific market. The market analysis consists of five different areas where information is collected and analyzed.

Market Description: Light up your market!

Define the market to be analyzed at the beginning and distinguish it as precisely as possible from other markets. Depending on the product or service, your market may be defined using a variety of criteria. In order to be able to carry out segment-specific analyzes, the target market is divided into different segments on the basis of specific properties. These characteristics may, for example, be sociodemographic (age, gender, income) or regional (districts, federal states).

The following questions should be answered in the market description:

- To which audience your product or service richet?
- Which age group is your product addressed to?
- What is the average income of your target group?
- Where do the players of your market live?

Find out as much specific information about your audience as possible:

- Does your target group like chocolate mocha or does she prefer black coffee?
- How fast is your target audience? Do you take 20 or 30 minutes for the coffee?

Market size and market development: How attractive is the market?

When determining the size of the market, you should use data that is as up-to-date as possible. The information ideally comes from the past quarter or year. This part of the market analysis is about identifying and assessing the actual sales or sales volume of a product or service in a particular market. Because based on the numbers, you can create forecasts of the market development and derive the attractiveness of the market. Market development includes market growth and growth rates.

3.2 What Are Suitable Sources Of Information?

The following administrations, as well as internet pages, provide free input for your market analysis:

- The Federal Ministry for Economic Affairs and Energy provides on its website information from A as automotive industry to Z as central innovation program middle class (ZIM) freely accessible.
- The task of the Federal Statistical Office is to provide and disseminate statistical information. These are objective and qualitative data from different areas such as B. Overall Economy and Environment.
- Statistics, market data, and studies can be found online at statistic statistics portal. There you can view data from market and opinion research instituions, information from the economy, and official statistics.
- Chambers of Commerce and Industry are cross-industry associations of self-employed and business enterprises. Detailed figures and statistics on specific sectors, can be found on the corresponding regional website, which can also be found on the roof portal of the Chambers.

Competitive Analysis: What are the characteristics of a market?

The competitive analysis looks at individual factors that are important for a market. Here the essential characteristics of a market are analyzed and described. The 5-Forces model has become established in the competitive analysis and, above all, in the consulting industry. The management theorist Michael E. Porter shows in which factors are important for the analysis of market and competition:

- **Bargaining power of customers:** How do customers react to price increases or decreases? How important is your product or service for your target group?
- **Bargaining power of suppliers:** Suppliers have particularly high bargaining power if the number of possible suppliers is limited. How can you possibly react to high price increases?
- **Replacement products in the market and competition:** Are there alternatives for your product or service? Could emerging innovation threaten the distribution of your offer?

- **New competitors and market entry barriers:** If a market is particularly attractive, new competitors often enter the market. What are the market entry barriers for potential competitors? For example, high investment costs for a product or service can be a market entry barrier. Access to a market is also made more difficult when high marketing costs are required to reach a certain level of awareness; resources are difficult to access due to exclusive suppliers, or business is decentralized.

Competitors on the market: what is the rivalry? Who dominates the market? Which competitors prevail and why?

In the competition analysis, you want to get to know not only your customers but also your competitors and possible competitive advantages:

- How soon should you enter the market?
- What dangers exist when entering the market?
- Who offers comparable products and how many competitors are there?
- What do your competitors do very well, and what can you do better?
- How much do your target markets resemble those of competitors?

Analysis of the customer industries

For the analysis of the customer industries, the sectors that achieve the highest sales or sales are highlighted. In doing so, you refer back to your defined market. Then you can analyze the structure and attractiveness of the industries in terms of different sales aspects. Because of your investigation, you will be able to reach the audiences of different industries and identify customer needs and behavior. Based on the results obtained, you can, for example, B. develop appropriate marketing strategies for your start-up.

These questions should answer the analysis:

- How high are the revenues generated in an industry?
- Which company is the market leader?
- Which trends does the industry currently exhibit?
- What innovations have been able to advance the industry lately?

Potential analysis of the target market: How will the market develop in the future?

In addition to the past and current state of the market, a market analysis also reveals a trend about its future development. For this purpose, the potential analysis highlights potential employees, market entry barriers, success factors, and current developments and trends. Especially for your sales planning and for possible investors, a prognosis of the market development is important.

Using market analysis, you can gain information about a particular market. If you are a start-up, want to explore your current market, or look at new markets, a market analysis can help you identify and weigh the opportunities and risks of a market. Based on market analysis, you can develop concrete marketing strategies and thus successfully implement your business idea.

CHAPTER 4: *PROFESSIONAL & PERSONAL SKILLS TO BE LEVERAGED.*

When a recruiter receives a curriculum, he looks at the professional experience or the training of the candidates, who are usually the first filter, and then goes on to look at other issues, such as the skills and aptitudes in the curriculum.

Skills and competencies are one of those aspects that we do not always pay attention to, but like any other point in our curriculum, it is a key aspect that we should deal with as tactfully as possible since it can have the key to Our curriculum exceeds the initial screening and call us for the interview, where we will insist on them.

Within "skills and competencies" you can enter practically everything, they can help you stand out in a curriculum without experience, without training or even without any of them; and we can even bet on a curriculum for competitions where these are the protagonists.

After all, having the skills and competencies necessary to carry out a job will always be more interesting than having great training but being unable to perform a job because you don't have those skills.

Next, we will know what professional skills and personal skills are, both equally important in our curriculum but with some differences that we should know, or we will explain how you can include your skills and competencies in the curriculum.

Another of the questions that you must solve before starting to make a curriculum vitae is the difference between skills and competencies, which although they are similar are different concepts that we cannot confuse, and less in the face of recruiters.

4.1 Professional skills vs. personal skills

It is not the same to speak of professional skills than to do a curriculum by competences, although they are intercommunicated and both should appear in our curriculum. But more than between the professional skills and personal competences of the curriculum, the most prominent difference can be found between soft skills and hard skills. We cannot be fooled by appearances since both are relevant even though the hard ones may sound more important.

Soft skills are those that can be useful to perform any job in very diverse fields. As we said, although the adjective "soft" may incite us to think that they are something secondary, they are highly valued since we talk about issues such as empathy, communication skills or self-confidence; a series of skills that facilitate teamwork, performance of tasks, work facing the public or that can be key in a meeting with a client and end up convincing him.

On the other hand, hard skills are those essential competences for a job, and it is easy that many times they appear among the requirements demanded by the company to the candidates that are submitted to the selection process.

They are usually professional skills that, depending on the sector in question, are related to production techniques, work tools used, etc. We talk about a wide range of possibilities, from the ability to repair a device to administrative skills.

Historically, it has given more relevance to hard competitions. However, with the passage of time and the search for more and more versatile and multidisciplinary workers, human resources managers are now more focused on soft skills than hard ones. This does not mean that we can omit the second of our curriculum, or that we do not pay as much attention as the soft ones since the balance is very even. Of course, when choosing a leader, soft skills are imposed by a win.

You must also keep in mind that each company is a world and that to occupy the same position in two different companies, one can opt for soft skills and the other for hard ones.

What you should keep in mind is that they are skills and abilities that fit what the company is looking for, what it demands in the job offer it has published, and you should make sure to include them as many skills as possible in the resume. Of course, you will not always have them all, but it is important to add as much as possible.

Among the most outstanding skills are those related to teamwork, the ability to make decisions or lead a team, knowledge and experience of the sector in which they work, the ability to negotiate, strategic thinking, the ability to adapt to the changes that may occur, the constancy in search of the results that allow us to meet the established objectives, the ability to communicate both in writing and verbally, etc.

How to include professional skills in the CV?

If we take a curriculum template, you will see that we do not find a specific section called "skills and competencies," unless you bet on the curriculum for competencies, which we will talk about later. This can make it difficult for us to add the skills to be highlighted in a CV since we will have to take advantage of the rest of the sections to show our skills and competencies to fill a job. For this, we will pay close attention to the keywords.

Many of the skills and abilities that you have will have obtained them through old jobs or in the classrooms, so when talking about your experience and training do not forget about the professional skills they have provided you . That is the time to insert those keywords that recruiters are willing to read, that ability that makes you a unique and ideal candidate to access a job. By introducing them here and not dedicating their own section, you also take advantage of them to gain space, something that we are not especially left over.

Of course, with languages and computer skills, we will make an exception. Languages and computer skills fall into the chapter of professional skills, are one of those skills to highlight in a CV and as you will know if we have a high level of a language should be highlighted as it deserves. The low or intermediate levels - up to B1 - can be added to the additional training, but from there we are facing an essential competition for employment, which can make us win whole.

Thus, in the language section, we will mention the different languages we speak, the level - if possible on the CEFR scale, from A1 to C2 - and we will add the official titles or courses that we have taken. In the chapter of the computer programs, we will highlight the apps and programs with which we are familiar, whenever possible, related to those required by the company in its job offer.

Before we said that there is the curriculum by competences. A CV format breaks with all the established schemes since it serves to give a leading role to the skills and competences against the role played by training and experience, which pass to a second term. In fact, in this type of curriculum, the section dedicated to work experience disappears in favor of another so-called professional skills and competencies, in which you can talk about your skills more freely.

Another way to highlight your skills and competencies is through the cover letter that you can attach to your resume. If you think they are not sufficiently reflected in the CV, you can add them to the cover letter, where we also have a little more freedom when talking about them, explain how you have acquired them, etc. The cover letter is a resource that we can never underestimate, and that can help us to value those skills and competencies that fit so well in the job we choose.

If you are able to reflect all your personal and professional skills, you will have made a complete curriculum, and practically unintentionally you will have put on the table a series of values that also interest recruiters.

Values such as honesty, character, humility, sincerity, coherence emerge from your personal skills ... This creates an almost perfect combination of skills and values, something that companies like since they try to associate their image with A series of values.

We have already said that what we cannot do is lie when talking about our skills and competencies, and the chapter on prohibitions is completed with generic and empty words that contribute nothing. Recruiters may expect the candidate to be defined as a skilled, thoughtful, intelligent or creative person, but when you are the one which includes these skills in your own curriculum, you show yourself too generic. You contribute nothing, and it is as if you had copied the skills requested in the job offer. You have to be more specific.

Example of skills for a CV

At this point, the difference between skills and competencies must be established. When talking about skills, we mean that the candidate is qualified to perform a specific task, and that is thanks to a skill acquired through his work experience, in the classroom or even in his hobbies. But if we go one step further, we find that competencies consist of putting into practice the knowledge acquired, integrating it into our way of acting to carry out the tasks we will deal with.

As a rule, skills are part of the skills, which are more generic. To better understand this difference between skills and competencies, we can follow the example of teamwork. The competition requires skills such as cooperating. If what you want is to play the leadership competence, you will need the ability to know the resources you have.

Sometimes, drawing the line that separates both concepts is a very complicated task. In this sense, if you choose to write a curriculum by competencies, you should not separate skills and competencies into two different sections, since doing so, you run the risk of being wrong. A good strategy to follow is to start talking about the skills and end the skills but without drawing a clear division. In addition, here you can include some of the references that you usually place in the section of other data of interest.

We have already talked about the skills most sought by companies, ranging from the ability to manage teams or negotiate to work in teams, analysis, assumption of responsibilities, etc. Another example of skill very well valued in a curriculum is discretion, something that you can also transmit through the values that your curriculum reflects, and that is essential when it comes to occupying positions of trust or where sensitive information is handled.

If you still do not know how to include your skills and competencies in the curriculum, you can look for examples in the curriculum vitae models, templates in which you will find the ideal place to include all your competencies. If you are one of those looking for examples of curriculum written on the web, do not forget that they are a good source of inspiration but you will have to adapt it to your person and the job offer to which you will respond.

Perhaps the skills and competences are the most complex aspect to deal with in a CV since there is no single formula to talk about them, not everyone has the same capabilities, and in each job offer, they will require different competences and skills. Remember that no matter how much you have a standard curriculum, you will have to adapt this small section every time you update it for a specific job offer, adding the key competencies that can be definitive for you to be called to the job interview.

CHAPTER 5: *HOW TO START A BUSINESS WITHOUT FAILING*

I think we are many who have ever thought of setting up something on our own, starting a business based on an idea that you have been thinking about for a while or just trying to launch something of yours, created by you, as your contribution to the world or your footprint on the planet.

Knowing how to start a business can be the purpose of life for many restless people who do not settle for a simple job in an organization.

Something that allows you to leave a gray job that does not give you much and let you live doing what you like, what motivates you and makes you happy.

Finding personal fulfillment through entrepreneurship is only one option, there are many other perfectly possible, each person is a world, but the reality is that we are increasingly looking for our transcendence through entrepreneurship, doing something we like, May we be well, that the world needs and also pay us for it.

I know very well that feeling and the illusion with which you imagine your new life by dedicating yourself to what you do well and making a living doing it.

But after that fleeting moment of lucidity and motivation, you return to the reality of your routine, and you will postpone any decision on what business to undertake, and that could change your life forever.

The most repeated phrase is "I don't have time now; I'll think about it calmly and see how I do it."

And so the days, weeks, months and years go by until another moment of inspiration comes to you, and you look back regretfully not having started your life change before and starting your business.

And you continue like this until you observe that time passes without realizing it and there is never going to be that ideal situation in which everything fits perfectly, and you finally decide to take the first step to undertake, the one that costs so much.

That is why now is the best time to ask yourself how long you will wait to reinvent yourself, whether it is to change your activity or work, to live the experience of how to start your own business or make decisions about what to do with your life.

I know that asking you that question may hurt you and that it is not easy to recognize it, but are you really going to continue to let your life go by without dedicating yourself to what you really like and make you happy?

Believe me, and I know how you feel; it has happened too many at some time.

I had recurring thoughts where great doubts assailed me about what I would really like to be doing with my life.

In my case, it was at 35 when I began to think too often about what I had done so far and so many things that I still wanted to do or undertake, and that was when I understood that I could not continue like this and that something had to change.

I knew that although I had a good job and I liked it, it wasn't enough, something was missing.

And I discovered that I lacked the most important thing to be motivated, a vital change that would direct my life by another path, a path with purpose, beyond a job that until now had worked for me to learn and grow. I knew I needed it, but I didn't.

These are the typical purposes that we think and aim year after year, and that accumulate in notebooks or get lost in the daily routine without becoming a reality.

And the main question that he repeated to me is, how long will I wait to take control of my life?

Because, although I had a seemingly successful life on a social and professional level, I was not really being faithful to my identity, but was living a replica of the lives of others, the life that society and circumstances had imposed on me and that I had accepted as normal.

And in your case, I hope you don't reach 40 to realize that you've let your best years go by without dedicating your life to a purpose or venture that truly fills you and makes you happy.

Think for a moment if any of this sounds to you:

- You know you need a life change
- Sometimes it frustrates you, and your work bores you
- You know you have talents in potency and hidden abilities
- You would like to dedicate yourself to what you like most and make you happy, but you don't know how to start
- You would like to undertake your ideas and be useful to society, but you do not dare to do so
- You get tired of seeing your best years go by and expect things to change alone

If you have identified with any of these phrases, believe me, that it is time to start something new in your life.

And do not see it as a problem, but as an opportunity for transformation to grow and live fully.

The main problem of many people is that they do not know how to start a business, what steps to take or just where to start, they are overwhelmed and prefer to stay as they are, which is the most comfortable and reasonable as we have been educated.

It is normal to see it that way, but don't worry, that in this section, I will tell you the exact system with the steps you need to take to discover who you are and start living on your talent, undertaking something you like and make you happy.

But first, you must understand that "not knowing what to do with your life" or "not knowing what to undertake or how to do it" is not really your problem.

Your real problem is that you don't know what you want because you don't know yourself enough, and you don't take the step to reinvent yourself because you don't know how to do it.

That is, your real problem is that you do not know the steps you need to discover who you are, connect your talent with your life purpose and use it to undertake with purpose, something that fills and motivates you.

I know many people who try again and again, some get it, and others don't.

But now I want to tell you what those who do get it do.

People are very similar in essence, and we always seek to be clear in our lives and find our way, the path of personal fulfillment and happiness.

Can you imagine for a moment getting it too?

Imagine living the life you dream of dedicating yourself to what you like and do best, and most importantly, adding value to others, being useful to society and feeling fulfilled.

Imagine for a moment connecting your talent with your life purpose and using it to undertake so many brilliant ideas that you have inside.

For all that is possible, everything is within you, in your ability to observe and learn, and in your freedom to decide.

Even if today you think you are not capable or think it is too late to change, believe me, that it is always possible.

But first you need to stop making up excuses and take action once, so let's go with the plan you should follow, in this order and without skipping any of the steps, okay?

Well, let's go with it, are you ready?

5.1 STEPS TO START A BUSINESS

This is the system that has worked for me and many people to go from "I don't know what to do with my life" to discover how to start a successful business.

Step 1: Know the reality of your current situation

We all have our own circumstances in life, they are unique and different, and each person is a world.

Do not compare yourself to anyone; do not suffer to see how others are and how are you, does not make much sense.

We all get our time for everything, do not get distracted, and go your way.

In this first step, you must analyze what is the situation that you are living in this moment of your life, with your work, your family, your friends, your health, your personal development, your concerns, your desires, your fears, etc.

And then you will imagine how you would like to be in a while, say a year, for example.

Describe it in detail, where you would like to be living, doing what, with what people, visualize it as if you could see and feel it.

Step 2: Find out who you really are

The second step is to discover who you are, that is, not what others say about you, but the person you are because of your origin and life experiences.

Discovering who you really are is going to give you the keys to how to start a venture.

Try to remember who he is and what is the boy or girl you have inside and what he has lived until you reach what you are today.

Do not judge him for what he did that does not matter, and if necessary, reconcile with him or her, keep in mind that he did the best he could at all times.

Review what your dreams are in life, what motivates you the most or limits you, your main achievements and your main frustrations, what your limits are and the things you can't stand, and finally describes what you feel most proud of, what they are your best skills and what do you think you should improve in your life.

Step 3: Define your identity

In the third step, you must define your identity based on the influences of your environment, those around you, your relationships, and your conversations with others.

Defining your identity, ideas for entrepreneurship will arise.

Try to take a tour of your life discovering what your memories of each stage are and identifying your values and beliefs, which are what make up your identity.

Something that can help you a lot is writing your own autobiography.

Believe me, and it is a very challenging and more difficult exercise than you imagine.

Sooner or later you will have to do it in your life, so the sooner, the better. You don't have to extend too much at the beginning, maybe one line or paragraph per year is enough?

Step 4: Connect your talent with your life purpose

This fourth step to start your business successfully is decisive because you must start to approach your talent, define it little by little and then connect it with your life purpose, what the Japanese call IKIGAI, the reason why you exist, the meaning of your life.

That purpose of life is where four fundamental areas converge, what you like to do, what you are good at doing, what the world needs, and what you could get paid for.

If one or more of them fail, you will end up having trouble making your business venture a reality.

That is to say, and when connecting your talent with your life purpose, you must bear in mind that you must add value to others, be useful to society in some way, and solve some kind of problem or need and that you can also make a living from it.

Step 5: Prepare for your independence

In the fifth step, you must change your dependent mindset to a self-sufficient or independent entrepreneurial mindset.

You can be dependent on a salary at the end of the month, or a job, or a relationship, or the help of your family, or comfortable circumstances that make you feel everything under control.

And with an independent mindset, you will understand that you depend on yourself and you will discover what your sources of motivation and energy are.

Knowing what really motivates you and what your goals in life are necessary to keep track of your goal and balance your inner saboteur, who makes excuses and limits you, with your inner superhero, your best version, of which you are most proud.

Step 6: Use your talent to undertake successfully

Only from this sixth step is when you can really consider the idea of the undertaking, and for this, what you have discovered in the 5 previous steps is fundamental, since now you can take advantage of your talent to undertake.

After discovering who you really are, defining your identity and connecting your talent with your life purpose, you will be in a position to understand if you have qualities to undertake, what type of entrepreneur you can be and what your strengths and weaknesses are.

No one is better than you to know how you will react to uncertain, changing, and unpredictable situations. Yes, welcome to the exciting world of entrepreneurship.

Step 7: Order your life and your mind before undertaking

Ordering your life and your mind before starting your business means asking yourself the big question:

Why do you want to undertake?

Because if the answer is simply to make money or succeed, we go wrong.

Never forget that your main reason for starting a business is to provide value to others, a lot of value, be useful to society, detect a problem or a need and provide your solution, in exchange for clear money.

I tell you this with forcefulness so that you do not get confused and have clear from the beginning what your superior purpose is when starting a successful business: impacting the world and leaving your legacy through a product or service that changes the life of the people for the better.

Only with that mentality will you be prepared to survive with passion and confidence to so many problems and obstacles that you will have to overcome.

Step 8: Transform your entrepreneurial idea into a startup

Now, you should be prepared to start the process of transforming your business idea into a startup, or what is the same, a new, emerging, uncertain company with limited resources.

In this step, you must identify which is the target audience, the niche market you want to address depending on the problem or need that your product or service will solve.

For that, you will have to design your empathy map where you describe what you see, what he hears, what he feels and what the avatar of your type client thinks, that is, put yourself in his skin.

Only after that empathy map can you define and validate your business idea before launching into the pool.

Step 9: The moment of truth

There is little left, and we are getting closer to the moment of truth where you will have to prepare for everything you will have to face when you need to defend your business idea and make it happen.

In this step, you will have to audit the 5 key aspects that will determine the success or failure of your business such as the team that you have started the adventure, the market you face, the business model to be profitable, the money you need to start working and how you plan to grow.

Step 10: The power of your story

And finally, and in my opinion, the most important step of all, you will need to tell your story and make yourself known by finding the keywords that define you and your project.

And believe me, it is not easy if you have not practiced it hundreds of times, yes, hundreds of times until you reach excellence.

You have to master concepts like Elevator Pitch and Pitch Deck.

Elevator Pitch is called that because it is time you have in an elevator, 1 minute, to tell someone quickly five things: who you are, what you do, who you do it, to achieve what, and through what.

Pitch Deck is a longer professional presentation, about 10 minutes, where you will have to explain in more detail and in a few pictures the problem you solve, what is the solution to the problem, your product, the market and the competition you face, the financial data, how you are going to grow and who you are the team among other things.

Well, now that you know the system, it is your decision to follow it to discover who you are, reinvent yourself and transcend by undertaking so many incredible ideas that I am sure you have inside, or continue as before, waiting for things to change alone.

How to take one business itself

If you want to take your idea of starting a business seriously, I invite you to this free webinar where in just over an hour I will tell you in more detail each of these steps.

"The system to discover who you are and undertake your ideas without making mistakes or wasting time."

I assure you that if you've read this far, this online workshop can change your life as it changed me years ago.

And if you stay until the end, I promise you a very special gift: The audit test for your business idea, with which you can review all the key points of your project to transform it into a viable business.

Today is the perfect day for you to make the decision to take the first step to transform your life and grow as a person impacting others, connecting with your talent and living on what motivates you the most and makes you happy.

I would like to convince you that at this precise moment in your life you have a great opportunity unknown to you, that you have hidden talents and abilities that are waiting for you to break your mental barriers and release your creativity to do something great at once.

This is the time to start wondering what you want to do with your life from now on, how you want to make sense of what you do every day, how to start your business and dedicate your life to what most fills you feeling fulfilled.

Conclusion

What will really mark your life is your attitude and the decisions you make freely, and even if you don't believe it, you are the only person responsible for your life, and as of today it is your decision to pursue what you want instead of hoping that Things change alone.

Undertaking something that matters is an option like so many others to feel fulfilled and do something with a purpose in your life.

But undertaking without first knowing you and knowing who you really are is a mistake.

Undertaking without a higher purpose is a mistake.

To start thinking only about money and not to add value to others is a mistake.

And I assure you that undertaking with a purpose is possible, that is precisely the difference between those who get it and those who do not.

And now tell me, can you imagine getting it too? What would your life be like?

I also imagined it, until I got where I am today, here, with you, sharing all this because life has taught me that:

- No one is better than anyone
- Everyone has their time and their moment in life
- No one is born knowing
- No one is born knowing their vocation and talent
- Everyone has had to learn and try many times until they can live on their talent
- They are normal people like you and me who connected with their talent and undertook their ideas

And the most important thing is that you can also get it.

All the people who get it have dedicated time and effort to get to know each other better and connect their talent with their life purpose, and they have followed a plan, a system, a process.

And I assure you that you are not different from others because deep down we all want the same, we all look for the same, leave our mark on the world, transcend in some way, feel that what we do has a meaning, do what we do most. We like it and see that it has a positive impact on others.

That is, to do something big each in their own way and at the same time earn a living to live autonomously and independently.

That is why, in this free webinar, I have decided to select and summarize the fundamental steps to help you in the way of knowing you better and undertaking successfully.

You can also get it, everything is inside you, and this is your new opportunity.

CHAPTER 6: *THE TOOLS, RESOURCES, AND MINDSET YOU NEED TO SUCCEED*

Never underestimate the amount of money you need to get started, the time it will take you to make a profit or have trouble working.

In your life, is one of your main goals to start your own business? Maybe building your own business has been part of your list of choices for a very long time? Do not start with your current employer; you have already heard of the success rate or lack of success for start-ups.

We all have the success rate of commercial failure engraved in our brains. According to the US Small Business Administration, 30% of businesses fail in their first year and about half of all convenience stores within five years. Only one-third of businesses will reach their tenth anniversary.

There are several reasons why many companies do not succeed. The main cause is the lack of profits and funding, which means underestimating the amount of money needed to finance a business. Does this mean that you should give up your dream? Not. But you need the right tools, resources, and state of mind before you embark on this new adventure.

Business creation, 101.

Starting a business is not easy, although it seems like a tedious job when accomplished entrepreneurs share their experiences. We hear about founders who seem to be quietly buying a website and turning it into a multi-million dollar business. In fact, starting a business involves careful evaluation, planning, and several financial and legal activities. Let's quickly recap the steps to take before starting your business:

Evaluate yourself: When thinking about what to do before starting a business, think about the skills and know-how you already have. As you examine what you are passionate about and the lifestyle you want to live - pause, ask yourself, "Why do I want to start my own business?"

Brainstorming Business Ideas: Start thinking about what's bothering you in the business world and how to fix it. Perhaps you have the knowledge or expertise to improve an existing business idea. Are you aware of trends, and do you always think ahead of the curve? Do you have skills that you can apply to a new or existing industry? These questions will help you find other business ideas.

Conduct a Market Study: Market research will tell you if it is possible to make a decent profit in different areas. Thorough exploration and analysis of your market will help you determine what gives your idea a competitive advantage over other areas and similar industries. If possible, give potential customers the opportunity to interact with your product or service so they can give you feedback.

Write Your Business Plan: Your business plan is a project that will guide you through the life of your business. In summary, discuss the purpose of your business, who your customers are, your long-term goals, and the financing of your business.

Make your business official: There are well-defined areas to keep for a solid company:

- Determine the structure of your business (LLC, company, or partnership).
- Give your business a name.
- Register your business in your state and at the federal level.
- Obtain a federal and state tax identifier.
- Acquire appropriate licenses and permits.
- Open a corporate bank account.
- Register for a trademark, copyrights or patents.
- Make sure you get legal advice if needed.

Choose a place of business: Thanks to the technology, and it is possible to start a business remotely, directly from home. For brick and mortar ideas, you'll want to think about demographics, accessibility, proximity to competitors, and the cost of rent and utilities.

Finance your business: How will you finance your business? You can cover the economic aspects of your new business in many ways, including saving money and financing the business yourself. Many ask for help from friends and family or get a grant or loan. Other options may be crowdfunding, stock trading, or working with Angel or Venture Capitalist investors.

Develop and improve your product or service: Solicit frequent feedback from your target audience to determine what they like and what they do not accept or will not accept. Hire specialists who can help you turn your dream into reality.

Your mindset is an essential ingredient for a winning company.

Unlike doctors, electricians, mechanics, and lawyers, there is no standardized test or certificate to announce that you are now ready to become a business owner. Even an MBA is terribly disappointing in his claim to business preparation. Although there are still classes that business owners will find helpful, finding the right ones may take some time.

Your university can give you the courses or courses and information you want in key areas such as accounting, marketing basics, finance, etc. However, the fact remains that as a business owner, you must develop the right mindset.

No matter your level of education, experience, or passion, having a winning entrepreneurial spirit will help you. Your mindset will make a difference in the way you run your business and make personal decisions. Mindset determines how you stand up, happy, motivated, and motivated.

The entrepreneurial equation.

According to Carl Roth, in his influential book The Entrepreneur Equation, here are ten states of mind that every entrepreneur should develop before starting his own business:

- **Evaluate your motivation:** Yes, it's your business. But you will have to respond to customers, partners, lenders, and investors.
- **Evaluate how you work with others:** Even if you are a solopreneur, you will still have to work with other people, such as accountants, lawyers, clients, and

freelancers. You will want to work together seamlessly with everyone in your new business; strengthen your communication and human relations skills.

- **Know Your Responsibilities:** Starting and running your own business is a job 24/7. Know how it will affect your personal life.
- **Sharpen your management skills:** You need to know how to manage your team to be more productive. In addition, you need to know how to interact and work with suppliers. Having experience in your area could help you.
- **It's not what you know, but who you know:** Take stock of your network of professionals. Think of people who can put you in touch with different business services, such as lawyers, investors, and lenders.
- **Be honest about your relationship with money:** Financial management can make or break your business. If you are a carefree spender, you will probably have cash flow problems. Take control here first - or you will spend more than what you bring.
- **Evaluate your personality:** Being a business owner means that you have to be flexible and ready to face the unexpected. If you are extremely stressed when things do not go as planned, running your own business will not match your personality type.
- **Examine your competitors:** A careful assessment of your competitors allows you to determine what sets you apart and differentiates you from other companies. This information and analytical thinking can be used to build your brand.
- **Test your scalability:** Successful business owners do not do everything themselves. They rely on automation and delegation. If your business decreases because you are not there, use your skills to succeed in your career. It's better to be successful than to be a bankrupt business owner, although you can "have" this passage to your belt too.

The best guides and entrepreneurial resources.

Starting and running your own business is not an easy task. You work hours, you face financial uncertainties, and you will put out many fires. To make matters worse, you probably do all this work by yourself.

The good news is that there is no shortage of guides and resources that can help you start and run your business.

General information:

US Small Business Administration: The American SBA is a must-have resource for business owners. Here you will find most of the information you will probably need. You will learn how to write a business plan, structure a business, register a business, and apply for a license.

Entrepreneur: Entrepreneur.com is a reputable publication that shares tips on starting and growing a business. Daily publishing guarantees popular, up-to-date articles and guides that cover everything from marketing to taxes to productivity.

Self Employed: Self-Employed.com is an excellent site where business owners can find advice on financing, taxes, and marketing for their business.

Financing

- ***Loans:*** If you need a loan, check out sites such as Kabbage, BlueVine, Fundbox, or Small Business Development Programs and Communities.
- ***Grants:*** For grants, resources such as the National Association of the Self-Employed and Small Business Innovation Research Program are some of your best options.
- ***Peer-to-peer leadership:*** Prosper and Funding Circle can put you in touch with peer-to-peer lenders.
- ***Crowdfunding:*** Crowdfunding your business? Start a campaign on Kickstarter or Indiegogo.
- ***How to Manage Money:*** Evergreen Small Business provides tips on how small businesses can track their finances.
- ***Legal:*** LegalZoom allows you to integrate your business and is affordable:

Rocket Lawyer allows you to create legal documents and ask questions to lawyers.

Nolo offers forms, as well as guides on the structure of your business.

The atrium is a new law start-up that helps small businesses. Help with everything that is legal.

Marketing:

Networking:

YEC can help you with professional networking. EO for the more experienced contractor. Be willing to help others.

Business Networking International (BIN) can help you get referrals by connecting with other businesses in your community.

SCORE is an organization that matches companies with volunteer mentors. This institution helps business owners to develop and grow their business. There are also online resources and online courses.

LinkedIn Small Business requires a subscription. Once joined, business owners can use LinkedIn to connect, promote, and network their activities.

Volunteer Match can locate volunteer opportunities in your community.

Your local Chamber of Commerce or Rotary Club.

The essential tools you need to start a business.

Finally, you must use the right tools to help you grow and maintain your business. Thanks to technology, these tools are affordable, easy to use, and can automate some of your most redundant tasks. Although the list is not exhaustive, here are some tools to consider. Personally, I use each of these tools, and I can say how incredible they are:

- Expensify can easily track your expenses.
- LivePlan can help you develop a solid business plan.
- WordPress is a free platform to create a personalized website.
- 99Designs is a great site to find designers for your logo or website.
- Fiverr and UpWork are great places to find talented freelancers.
- Aweber and MailChimp can be used to generate leads and conduct an email marketing campaign.
- Hootsuite and Buffer automate your efforts on social networks, planning publications in advance, and interacting with subscribers.
- Due or QuickBooks can make your accounting as simple as possible.
- TurboTax allows you to do your professional and personal taxes yourself.
- Trello is a project management system that allows you to assign and guide tasks.
- G Suite is the foundation of your business and comes with Gmail and Drive.
- HubSpot is an all-in-one marketing platform provided with CRM, marketing, and sales suites.
- Google Adwords and Facebook ads can market your business online.
- Google Analytics provides demographic and behavioral information about your audience, as well as information about marketing efforts.
- With Calendar, you can share your calendar with others and use machine learning to receive smart planning suggestions.
- G2 helps you in all the reviews of your business.
- Intercom helps you discuss and market strategically with your potential customers.
- For customer service, use Survey Monkey and FreshDesk.
- LastPass remembers and stores all your passwords.
- Stay in touch with customers and virtual workers via Zoom, Lifesize, Slack, and Skype.
- Gusto manages your needs in human resources and personnel.

There are so many variables that you will have to face when setting up your new business. Go to your business, knowing that you can do everything right and always arrive in the short term - with failure. There are things you cannot possibly prepare for. Even these things will make you sleep at night, and they will give you experience for your next turn.

Become hard; opt for your new business with everything you have and do not hesitate. You will have a lot of success in building your business - but nothing is worth doing without effort.

The stage of the quantification of trigger needs is crucial in order to nde measure the profitability of your project, n to validate the main strategic choices, n reduce the risks of failure, n try you in your future role of decision-maker, nde show the seriousness of your project to your funders and partners.

6.1 Changes In Mentality You Need To Move From Freelancer To CEO

Albert Einstein once said that it was impossible to solve a problem with the same level of consciousness as the one who created it. According to the same principle, your business will not evolve if your state of mind remains the same.

Many entrepreneurs I have worked with over the years have started providing service to their clients. This is one of the quickest ways to gain ground because the overhead is minimal and you just need a laptop, a smartphone and a powerful Wi-Fi signal to make a photo six figures in a Parisian cafe.

But new challenges arise as soon as you start earning more than $ 100,000 a year. Between $ 10,000 and $ 20,000 a month, you fall into the "quicksand." The more you kick, the more difficult it will be to walk to keep your head out of the water.

You are exhausted and do all the work in the company, even if you know that you need help. You cannot maintain this rhythm forever, and this is already starting to show in your work.

You now have an important decision to make: are you going to remain a freelancer, or are you going to make the jump to the CEO? If you choose the new path, the trip will be difficult but extremely rewarding. To do this, you will have to radically change your mentality.

Here are three key principles that you need to internalize in order to move from freelancer to CEO.

Performance, not hours.

CEOs are paid for the performance of their system and not for the time spent indoors. Freelancers trade time for money and find themselves trapped in a house that collapses when they stop laying bricks.

As soon as they stop working, the money stops going. It's the description of a job, not a business. When every dollar you earn is tied to the time you spend working, it stops you from living your life.

This is not the CEO's way. CEOs, on the other hand, use the time of others to create money.

The CEO does not "work" for money. Tasks and "work" are at stake, but the CEO's income depends on how well she has designed her systems, people, and processes. If the system is efficient and scalable, it can exponentially generate more money as the organization and demand for the product increases.

Think of it this way: in the beginning, your business is a system that uses your time and energy in a cost-effective way. It works on a small scale, but your time and energy are limited, so at some point, you maximize (if you try to oversize, it's when you're exhausted). The real problem is neither your work ethic nor your productivity. - This is how you have (or have not) designed the system.

No direct amount in dollars per hour can be allocated to a CEO's job, as his work is the culmination of every element of the system he has designed to create the product.

They are paid for results, not for completed tasks. CEOs are composers who orchestrate a symphony that is their company and money is music to their ears.

CEOs know their numbers and manage their resources like a pro.

If I asked you what your profit margins are, could you tell me? And if I asked you what your closing ratio was, how much of your gross income went to operating expenses or what was the average value of your customers?

Most freelancers do not know their numbers. Period.

Freelancers are used to having their personal and business finances mixed. They see the money they earn as their money to spend and do it freely. (I'm not criticizing, I was like that too.)

This way of thinking is the root of the "broken millionaire syndrome."

CEOs realize that money is the fuel of travel. To steer the ship in the right direction, you have to look at your business objectively. And the numbers never lie.

Not knowing the numbers of your business is like flying in a plane without a dashboard. You go very fast, completely blind. Not good.

Numbers allow you to track performance against goals, empower yourself and your team, and spot weaknesses before they become big problems. CEOs know their numbers. Do you?

CEOs know that their job is to elevate others to leadership.

Most freelancers are used to being the "best" to solve problems and have learned to depend on themselves. Because let's face it, most people are dead in their work.

In basketball, freelancers would be ball hogs. They live according to the following saying: "If you want something to be done well, do it yourself." This state of mind is first a force because it creates momentum and fast action that leads to results. But in the long run, the "doing it all" approach to the business game is a hindrance to the freelancer because it does not allow him to put others in a leadership position.

You do not have to be the only superhero in your business. You should focus on recruiting superheroes. It means allowing people to integrate and make their own decisions, teaching them to make the right choices based on the values shared by all members of the organization.

When your team knows what to do without asking, can make important decisions and implement action plans without having to clarify all the details, you have really created leaders. Leaders continue to make mistakes, but they also take responsibility for these mistakes and can count on them to learn from them.

A good CEO learns what Gino Wickman calls "delegation and elevation." They realize that they are very rarely the best candidates for the job; they cannot wear all the hats or be everywhere at once. So, rather than focusing on the work themselves, they focus on selecting the right person to do the work and allow it to lead.

To create a company is to mobilize means to provide an object or a service, the goal being to suit the customers while being competitive. These means are often expensive and require funding. It will also fund communication efforts to publicize the offer. Yet some founders manage to settle from scratch, or almost.

CHAPTER 7: *HABITS THAT PREVENT YOU FROM BEING A MILLIONAIRE*

If you have some customs like these, how do you intend to become a millionaire? Here we tell you the practices that you should abandon. Most of us, including you, have bad habits that get in the way along this path. If you are able to give up the following habits, you should be able to understand that becoming a millionaire is not an idea as far from reality as you think. We all want to be.

For me, as for many other people, these habits were what prevented me from becoming a millionaire:

1. Sleep when you shouldn't

If you get up until noon and work 12 or more hours per day to compensate that you started late. Here is the thing. I understand perfect because I struggled with that for years. Not all of us are active people in the morning. I still stay in bed during the cool and rainy mornings.

Successful people are known for waking up early, usually before everyone in their home, so they can start work early, catch up on the news, respond to emails and exercise without sacrificing the time they spend. They spend with their family.

2. Neglect your health

When you're not healthy, you're tired, less productive, more stressed, and much more likely to get sick. How can you focus on building your health, if you fight against these factors every day?

3. Do not read

People with money, invest their time and effort needed to expand their knowledge, keep up with the news and trends within their industry, learn from others, and take charge of continuing to innovate.

Reading brings different perspectives, and it allows you to obtain several points of view that in turn will expand yours, giving you the necessary push to dream big and motivate you to never give up.

4. Depend on a single source of income

People with a lot of money have several sources of income. Which means that for those of us who aspire to wealth, we have to invest part of our income in paying our debts, and reserve for retirement and invest.

This does not mean that you have to get a second job while you wait for results (it is not a bad idea until you have a better option). It could be something you are passionate about, such as writing about technology. You can do it through a blog and start earning passive income through the market.

5. Do not set a budget

Everyone needs to create a budget and adhere to it, but, unfortunately, there are many people who do not. Since they cannot see if they are spending more than they earn exactly, it often brings them financial problems. If you notice that this is your case, then you need to start reducing unnecessary expenses, and you should speak with an advisor to claim you.

In fact, this is another habit discovered by millionaire authors such as Thomas Stanley and William Danko after analyzing millionaire people for their book The Millionaire Next Door.

6. Do not think ahead

In my study, ninety-five percent of poor people did not save, and most of them accumulated debts to subsidize their quality of life. Consequently, they have no money either at the time of retirement nor for the education of their children, not even for opportunities that arise.

Not saving and spending more than you earn generates long-term poverty without the hope of escape.

7. Do not pay attention to small expenses

You may think that spending $40 a day on a cup of coffee has no effect on your purse. The same goes for that $500 gym membership that you almost never use. But, although in the scheme of things these are small expenses, even if you don't believe it, they add up quickly.

Recently, I randomly reviewed my company's credit card payments. I discovered that 35 percent of people who buy coffee at least 4 times a week or who go to the cafeteria every day, only pay the minimum of their credit card monthly.

Again, for this reason, the budget is so useful. It helps you manage these small expenses so you can adjust and focus on the important things. Remember to just keep the subscriptions you really use.

8. Go out with the wrong people

Replace the toxic and negative people in your life with those who are optimistic, who motivate and support you. "In life, you will only get success if you surround yourself with the right people.

9. Postpone

One thing is to say that you want to become a millionaire and another very different is to start doing it. If you want to get out of the financial stagnation, then you need to take action as soon as possible. If you sit down with a financial professional to adjust your budget, this would be a great step to start doing instead of talking.

10. Drink and bet

There is nothing like getting rich quickly"; "Financial success takes time, initiative and requires a relentless effort"; "Those who bet, fool themselves into thinking that there is a shortcut to success.

Instead, millionaires "create the habit of pursuing their dreams and their goals."

On the other hand, excessive alcohol consumption prevents you from becoming a millionaire since it impairs your memory, the ability to think clearly and your health. That does not mean that occasionally you cannot drink a glass of wine or a beer. Don't make drinking a habit.

11. Watch too much television

Rich people have small televisions and large libraries. Poor people have small libraries and large televisions.

Do not misunderstand. I like to watch Netflix from time to time. But, as in the discovery of Corley, the rich prefer to read, exercise or educate themselves instead of wasting time watching television. Making productive use of time is a hallmark of millionaires. Wasting time is for poor people.

12. Do not find a mentor

I am sure that if I had found a mentor years ago I would have become rich ever since. Why do I believe it? I could have learned from the successes and mistakes of someone who has developed in those fields, his advice could have helped me to omit so many mistakes that I have experienced and instead I could have obtained some benefit.

Instead of going out to get a mentor, open your eyes, they are around you. You can take the advice of a university professor or your parents.

13. Stay in your comfort zone

Taking risks and leaving your comfort zone is disturbing. I get it. But until you make that leap you will find financial success. This habit worked very well for Bill Gates, Richard Branson, Larry Ellison and Warren Buffet.

The pursuit of wealth requires risks, most people do not, so they are not rich.

14. Do not ask questions

You do not know everything. For a moment set aside your ego. I hate being the bearer of bad news, but that is a fact and will prevent you from being rich until you face it.

I learned the hard way that was trying to guess the future leads to failure and making bad decisions. If you are not sure about an investment or an idea for your business, do not hesitate to ask for feedback and advice.

15. Be consumed by failure

Entrepreneurs wear failure as a badge of honor. That does not mean they enjoy or want to fail. Conclude a business and lose almost everything is rubbish, but those blows of life are necessary to become as strong as possible.

Do not get confused. The failure is horrible. But you shouldn't let that stop you. Take risks, and, if you fail, learn from your mistakes and move on.

16. Do not set daily goals

One of the best habits I adopted during the last years was to write my goals every day and early in the morning. This inspires me and encourages me to achieve my goals.

I discovered that setting daily goals helps prioritize from the most important to the least important. For example, instead of looking for my overdue bills of $ 100, I focus on one or two at $ 1,500. Prioritizing means doing what really matters.

17. Think negatively

Long-term success is only possible when you have a positive mindset," writes Corley.

These are some examples of the most common negative thoughts we have and that most can overcome:

- **Doubt yourself.** Training, education and a mentor can change this thinking.
- **Believe that your goals cannot be achieved.** Focus on achieving your daily goals and driving yourself.
- **Have bad grades.** No. Grades and learning difficulties do not determine success.
- **The competition is too tough.** You will never know until you try. And, in the worst case? Just turn around.
- **Lack of concentration.** A healthy life and set daily goals can keep you focused.

18. Don't save

A job will never make you rich. Nor will you save all your money in a piggy bank. So how do you build wealth?

So how is it achieved? Through material assets such as a profitable business, a portfolio of growing shares or investing in real estate law.

Remember, your car and your toys are responsibilities that take away the income of your future wealth. Focus on acquiring things that will give you money in the long run.

19. Create excuses

Excuses were one of the biggest obstacles between wealth and me. Creating excuses is easy when we are trying to understand why we have so many debts and if we don't have a six-figure income. To say that we want to "live in the moment" is an excuse for not working and creating a better future. Stop making excuses and start working.

For example, do not worry about saving when you are drowning in debt. Pay first, and that way you can start saving and investing. If you don't earn enough money, look for another source of income such as selling things online or delivering pizzas. That won't solve all your problems, but at least it's a start to get rid of excuses.

20. Do not follow Rule 70/30.

After paying your taxes, learn to live with 70 percent of your income for your needs and luxuries," "it is important to see how you allocate the remaining 30 percent after that.

Giving a third to charity, a third to capital investments and the last third to savings. You will not notice anything at first, but let five years go by and the differences will be noticeable. 10 years later, they will be completely solid.

CHAPTER 8: *HOW TO TRANSFORM YOUR PASSION INTO A SOURCE OF INCOME*

What is a passion?

For many, passion is an intense emotion that leads strongly towards an idea, object, theme, person, etc.

Passion comes hand in hand with enthusiasm, admiration, interest, among other desirable side effects.

Imagine creating a lifestyle around what you like most.

Finding your passion has to do with your heart and what you love, it is simple for those who know each other well and recognize what we love to do. Finding our passion and working on it requires self-knowledge, self-esteem, wisdom, courage, and coherence. Almost nothing.

Passion = Income

To begin in the search for your passion, you must first ask yourself, why do I want to find my passion in life?, and the answer is very simple: but what the hell will you do with it? The only purpose for which we exist is to love, wake up from sleep. Point

But what steps can you follow to recognize your passion:

Ask yourself what motivates you, what moves you, and based on this question you can have a broader picture of your aspirations. There are different factors that can motivate us, identify them, analyze situations in your life where to see what your motivations were, self-assessment is an excellent practice to recognize your passion

Follow the hunch. When we feel attraction, we are almost never wrong. Explore it I believe that the hunches are ours speaking to us about what we should or should not do, and who better than your real self to take their revelations ... follow your hunches, follow your heart and you will find your passion.

Do not make money your main engine. A serious mistake of many people is to confuse their passion with the love of money, and could not be considered love, rather attachment to money. If you confuse your passion with making money, you will fail: Who only seeks money ends up not making money. Follow your passion, and if you do it professionally, your passion will lead you to lots of money.

Do not fear "failure." Failure does not exist, it is an unconfirmed story. There are many people who, for fear of failing in the search for their passion, prefer to continue in a comfort zone, a known area, instead of entering the unknown in order to find themselves. Serious mistake, depriving oneself of self-awareness out of fear is just an illusion. Rest assured that you are such an exceptional being designed for success and get what you want.

Be patient, and put dedication to all the work you do, be disciplined to get everything you want, be patient to infinity and know that things are already developing on a plane that you cannot see. Be certain that everything is working in your favor. Learn to appreciate every moment, if you are impatient it is because you are not sure, and if you are not sure, you deny it. Do not be fooled by the mind, by the ego, try to be present, only then you will not have impatience.

Do not get carried away by others. Friends, family, couple ... they will tell you what you have to do, they will recommend or advise you on what you should work on and what not. I am going to give you some advice, follow your heart, not your advice, thank the intention, but show them what your life is, only you will be able to recognize your passion. No one else will tell you where it is, only your heart. They can't tell you what path you should take, because nobody else can do this job for you.

You can also ask yourself what others want you could offer them. Serve and you will serve yourself.

Do not seek your passion for alien recognition, it is not a therapy. And do not let money be your main engine, I find what motivates you and do it without fear, do not fear failure, because failure as such does not exist, it is only a valuable experience for your learning, find what you love and work hard in it, with love, with motivation. Success, recognition, money, peace, everything, absolutely everything will come in addition if what you do, you do with love.

Following the steps of what you love can never be a failure, it is pure coherence.

8.1 Ideas To Turn Your Passion Into Extra Income

When we discover what we are good for and what are those things that we are passionate about in life is like starting to live. It is possible that you are already clear about what it is that motivates you to get up and what you would do even if you are not paid, perhaps, write or work as a volunteer, politics, maybe do some crafts, I do not know, but you do. Now it only remains that you dive deeply into that passion and analyze if you can turn it into some extra income that will help balance your budget.

If you have a fixed income I do not recommend that you leave it to venture to make your passion produce money, my recommendation is that you take part of your free time to channel that passion into something that can generate some extra income.

In this chapter, I share with you some ideas of how you can turn that passion into a new source of income or why not, into a new profession.

The first step is to commit to follow your passion and take action...

1. Create a blog

Being a blogger offers you a great variety of advantages if you are passionate about any specific topic. The best thing is that the time you will invest is flexible, because you can work very easily from the comfort of your home with just one computer. You can write almost anything you can imagine. Today there are sites like WordPress and Blogger that are not so complicated to start.

Although I tell you that it is easy to start a blog, do not misunderstand me, it takes a lot of work and skill to be successful. As your success is in what you write, you must be careful with your grammar and follow a logical progression, which can keep people with similar interests connected. You should know how to market yourself and maintain the focus and determination to continue with your blog even when things do not go as you want.

To have a successful blog, the main fuel is that your passion is strong enough that you feel motivated to write about that topic with some frequency. If so, you will make your passion become extra income by being a blogger.

2. Offer to tutor

If you are passionate about teaching others and have patience, this is a good opportunity to generate extra income. For example, if you can play an instrument, you are good at math, you can turn your passion into extra money for your pocket. Another way to do this is to look for a community center where you earn a fee and can teach any talent you have to other people. This ability can also be offered online, to give personalized tutorials or through videos.

Pay attention to the comments of others, especially when they admire you for some skill you have, sometimes they are the ones who tell us what we are good for and want to learn from us, who knows and becomes future clients.

3. Take photos and sell them

If your passion is to go out with a camera to capture unforgettable moments, this can put money in your pocket, because you can sell the photographs in agencies that are intermediaries between you and the client that needs an exclusive photo for their advertising campaigns as for their websites and that instead of paying high sums of money directly to a photographer they buy them on some website like:

- ***istockphoto,*** is one of the most renowned pages, if you place your photos here you can earn 20% of each photo you sell or 40% if you only place your photos with them.
- ***Shutterstock:*** It is one of the best options to sell your photographs online, despite not having so many visits. What makes it different is that customers become members and have the opportunity to download a certain amount of photos for a monthly fee and each time they download one of them they will pay you between 25 and 30 cents for each of them.
- ***Dreamstime:*** This agency is one of those that offer the greatest benefits when it comes to selling your photos, pays excellent 50% commissions for each photo sold and if your images become popular they pay extra bonuses.

These are only three, but there are many other agencies that offer these services through the internet, do not stay with those beautiful photos stored on a computer, place them in one of these sites and make them generate extra income for you.

4. Create videos

If you are passionate about creating videos, pay attention and start recording attractive videos, the ones that generate the most attention are those that follow the same theme. Then you upload them to YouTube for example, you place ads and every time people see the ad in your video they pay you some money, imagine if they go viral and many people see them, it will be a good extra income.

For example, if you are passionate about exercising, you can record routines that can help other people. Or if you know how to organize the house, if you like flowers and know how to create beautiful gardens, you can also do it. This applies to almost any passion you have. The following is to market your video by sharing your link with the people you know, social networks, bloggers interested in your topic, etc.

5. Freelance

In addition to blogs, there are other ways to work online from home, including: Writing articles, doing translations, transcriptions, being a virtual assistant, designing web pages, etc.

If you realized that you are good at writing, write fast or know a little English, do not wait and register on one of the websites such as upwork or workana among others, which offer these services to your customers and you can get contracts.

6. Create crafts to sell

If you are good at crafts, you can identify some stores in your city and ask that they allow you to display your products in exchange for a portion of the profits. You can also make yourself known through social networks or sell your products through a website. Your success will revolve around building relationships so that your product acquires more value.

I have only shown you some ways by which you can turn something you are passionate about into an extra income generator for you, but there are many more.

CHAPTER 9: *IT IS TIME TO BUILD YOUR OWN DREAMS!*

Life is full of mysteries and one of the most disturbing, is when two or more people who pursue a common goal, manage to coincide in time and space ; and the ability to recognize these people is one of the most important tasks for every entrepreneur. Hence the importance of selling the dream ; that is, to tell others, that goal or desire we pursue, that dream that we are building, hoping to find an echo, in some other dreamer, with whom we can make synergies and guide our entrepreneurial actions towards a common purpose.

We have stated that it is success, it is an achievement achieved, although it would be more accurate to say, "a shared achievement", since no one can claim the exclusive merit of his achievements; Somehow, directly or indirectly, they are a hundred and up to thousands of people who can participate in a process culminated in a successful experience. In that sense, the entrepreneurial process must be a catalyst for talents, initiatives, ideas, ventures, of course, led or driven by someone.

A few years ago, we started in the city of Cali, (Colombia), an entrepreneurial experience, which we call the network of friends; it is born out of necessity, to respond to the community that faced the employment deficit; that we solved it in a simple way, "if you don't get a job, get to work"; implying that, although there is a deficit in employment, there is also a surplus of work, this, many options to undertake. Everything is in the mental attitude towards the crisis. It is understandable that there are unemployed, which is due to a socio-economic situation, but it is inadmissible, that there are unemployed, which is due to a situation of the socio-cultural order.

The objective of the network of friends is to build a community of support and commercial cooperation, in which enterprises and businesses are promoted, working with philosophy, “I have what you need; you have, what I or someone else needs. ”In this sense, the network of friends becomes a model of associativity, whose social goal is summed up in a slogan,“ Doing business is building the country. ”This experience of Entrepreneurship has led us to understand the importance of joining efforts and wills, sharing knowledge and experiences, and projecting oneself towards common goals. In this process of promoting entrepreneurship, we have identified five (5) enterprising actors or agents, who are present, in the construction of dreams:

- Who has the idea
- Who structures the idea
- Who manufactures or builds the idea
- Who promotes or sells the idea
- Who sponsors the idea
- Who manages and executes the idea
- Who benefits from the idea

Who has the idea?

He is the dreamer or visionary; that person who conceives a business possibility from a latent demand or need, imagines a potential market for his idea, which in some cases, can be conceived as a dream. Different authors agree that the world belongs to dreamers, those who anticipated future realities, conceiving possible scenarios. What we find every day, at another time, might seem crazy and irrational. Fortunately, the dreamer and visionary, was willing to believe in his idea and fight to make it happen. In our work as business advisors, we have met hundreds of people, thinking geniuses who have not been taken seriously, by those who consider them a bit crazy, and have not given them fair credit. What does a dreamer need? Someone who credits your idea and gives you support to make them happen.

Who structures the idea?

It is the job of the mentor, business advisor, corporate advisor; who has the virtue of being interested in the entrepreneur; first in him, as a person; second, in his entrepreneurial idea. A mentor is the one who puts at the service of others his knowledge and experience to give lights that illuminate the path by which the entrepreneur must lead. It provides support and accompaniment, advises on the march and helps the person to carry out their own process of continuous improvement and scope of achievements. The mentor's greatest contribution is to the person of the entrepreneur, who must be able to develop his full potential as he moves forward in his life project.

Who manufactures or builds the idea

That person who enjoys technical expertise; not necessarily the dreamer or visionary; not the mentor; and this opens the way to the participation of other people who have the knowledge and expertise. At different times of our life, we will have genius in some art or trade, which will be key in the manufacture or structuring of the idea. The dreamer, from the hand of his mentor, has a general idea, but it is the technician who gives him shape and body; making a concrete and moldable product. One of the most rewarding experiences, for those of us who move in the world of design, creativity and ideas; is to find that person, a genius of crafts, crafts, art and technique, that is able to put skin to our initiatives and shape a sketch. And most admirable,

Who promotes or sells the idea

That person, who articulates our idea to the commercial dynamics, to the demand supply system and achieves, whether the desired product, that someone is willing to acquire it, as a personal good. While sales, it is the universal profession, and whatever profession, trade or activity we develop, we must exercise in the sales universe; Not only sell our products and services, but above all, be able to sell ourselves. It is a work that we must develop; and it is one of the secrets of successful entrepreneurs; in spite of the belief that some people may have, of considering that they are not good to sell; That is not his forte; that they perform better in other areas; and that may be true; however, two phenomena can happen: First, the person, due to their beliefs and fears, He hasn't let the giant that lies asleep inside him wake up. Second, even if the person is not the sales genius, he must be convinced of what he does, and the convinced one convinces. Who better than the author of the idea to explain it? Who better than its creator to explain its genesis, development and transcendent purpose? So, all without exception, we must exercise in the world of sales, without forgetting that we need to have experts and specialists to fulfill this task that is definitive for the success of any business. Whoever promotes the idea must develop strategies for the whole process, since the idea is conceived, launched and supported. In this sense, advertising is a basic tool and a great strategic ally.

Who sponsors the idea?

There are two ways to sell an idea: On paper, or as a finished product. In both cases a seller is required, not only of services or products, but above all of the dreams. We saw, as life, mysteriously allows in the path of dreams, several people who follow a similar path, coincide. And it is wonderful, when they agree, who has an idea, with that person who has the ability to sponsor it. Usually, dreamers are rich in ideas, (at least in the beginning) but not necessarily in financial resources, so it is necessary, to sell their ideas to others, with the ability to leverage their dreams, with whom they should make synergies A dream sponsor, thanks to your investment, get the dream placed wheels. The idea ceases to be a scheme or sketch, to become a real product.

Who manages and executes the idea

That person who makes sure, that the idea, in addition to being realizable and realizing, is profitable. It is possible that there are creative, charismatic, influential, persuasive, effective entrepreneurs, administrators, leaders; but it is not the rule. It is not common for a single person to gather all the skills and talents, but a team can settle for people who contribute their predominant competence. In this sense, it is essential for the idea to thrive and progress entrepreneurship, there are a judicious administration and efficient management of resources. A good administrator is one who enjoying autonomy and time; He knows that on the day he must report, he must have everything up to date, in order and report positive results. An administrator doesn't know them all either. Therefore, it must rely on other people who have legal, technological, and computer knowledge, depending on the nature of the business. The virtue of good administrators is that they manage to increase profits, and not just conserve resources.

Who benefits from the idea?

Those people or community that will be directly benefited; although all those who are part of the group of stakeholders in which the idea works, and the project thrives, are benefited. But, it is necessary to emphasize, in the end user, in that subject that inspires the idea, by virtue of their needs, tastes, preferences, projections and potentialities. It is precisely this end users, who validate and legitimizes the idea, with their satisfaction and complacency.

The entrepreneur is not a kind of Leonardo Da Vinci, with a great report of skills and abilities; but you must have the ability to build relationships with other entrepreneurs that accompany you, in building a shared dream. And this is based on our thesis, that success is not an exclusive achievement of a person, but a shared achievement, in which much more participate, inspired and motivated by the dream or the idea that is born in an entrepreneur's mind.

9.1 Ways To Create The Life Of Your Dreams

Imagine working on what you want, driving the car of your dreams and having the house you like. Wouldn't it be a utopia?

Imagine working from wherever you want to work, driving your favorite car and living in the best cities. Wouldn't it be the life of your dreams?

In this world we have an abundance of opportunities that can give you the wealth, joy and satisfaction you desire. If you are looking to create the life of your dreams, you must be prepared to do things that others do not want.

After hearing hundreds of personal stories this year, I have realized that there are many people who lead a lifestyle that they did not choose. Most of them have the potential to change, but they don't do it out of fear. They want a glamorous life, but they lead an existence of denial.

Do we all want to have money? Yes! And many more important things too. We want love, romance and adventure. Many also seek peace and tranquility. Others struggle to contribute to certain parts of the world and leave an eternal mark on people who can help. Some more just want to be recognized for what they do.

Whatever your dream, you can achieve it. Many people agree that the only thing they truly want from life is happiness. Here are 10 ways to create the life of your dreams.

1. Find your passion

No matter who you are, there is a perfect job for you. If you are still looking for your passion, ask yourself "What would you be willing to do without pay for six months?" The answer will surprise you. If you already know what it is, then do it well and find a way to turn it into your career.

A friend of mine was tired of working in jobs with no future, so he bought a sketchbook. He didn't know that art was his passion, especially since his third-year teacher told him that he "didn't know how to draw." Now he makes oils for which he earns very well.

2. Develop your vision

Your ideal lifestyle is directly related to the vision you have of yourself in the future. Do you want to improve your lifestyle? You must imagine what you want before you get it! What are you willing to do today to have a better tomorrow?

Many lifestyles are built on frustrations of the past.

3. Be patient

Life is about being patient because everything we do requires it. Some of our deepest desires are the result of patience. However, it is not always easy to wait. Many times we see that others get results faster than us when we should not compare ourselves to others.

What was created for you will eventually come to you. Do not worry about tomorrow, but what you have to do today. If you have a clear vision of what you want to happen, stay motivated and keep the faith. Without it, nothing is possible. Believe in your dream and be patient.

4. Love others

Love is the most powerful force on Earth. Nothing can happen without its power. We are all connected by love and nobody can live without him. Think of the people you love. Do you know how much they impact you every day? Do you know how much you impact them every day?

The only way to give you an idea, however dark it may seem, is to imagine what your funeral would be like. Imagine hearing what people would say about you. It would be much better than you imagine! If you take this perspective and live your life as if every day will count to make others happy, you will lead an existence where you have everything to gain and nothing to lose.

5. Be humble

This is one of the virtues necessary to create a great lifestyle. Having a humble existence means being connected with who you really are, your dreams and where you are going. By doing this, you will be able to show others that you are interested in their feelings.

Remember, humility is not false modesty. Many people reject generous favors because they feel they don't deserve them. Humble people know how to receive as much as they know how to give. In fact, the only way to give is to receive to the extent that is fair.

6. Raise your voice

There are many times when you will have to talk to defend yourself. Many of us have been silent when we wanted to talk about our feelings. We need to articulate our thoughts and make our voice heard. If we don't talk, we can fall into rage and pain, which deteriorates our peace of mind.

The next time you have to raise your voice to defend yourself, don't be afraid to do it. Without being rude, you can tell people that you deserve respect. Sharing your thoughts and feelings will allow you to change behaviors. Say what you think and believe in what you say. Let your words make an impact.

7. Trust others

There is nothing better than operating in an environment of trust. Culture is everything. If you are in a place where people betray each other with gossip, even in the smallest way, then it is time to change direction. You cannot compromise the trust that others have for you.

Those who have relationships full of trust can change the course of their lives. You should be able to see around you people who energize and empower your dreams and goals. Also, if you can trust yourself, you can trust others.

8. Ask for help

Your life will be much simpler if you get used to asking for help. Some time ago I helped an executive become CEO of his company. His problem was not his ability or his talents, but his inability to go to his team. Learning to recognize that he couldn't do it all just changed his life.

What you do today could be done by other people? If there is any area of your life that could be improved, it is probably because you are not asking for the right help. It is time to face the truth and trust the support of others. You will find that people are more willing to support you than what you are willing to ask for support.

9. Contribute

How much do you support the community? All your material wealth is the reflection of what you give to society. If you want to improve your lifestyle, you must find a way to increase your impact on the world. Your impact equals revenue. The more you facilitate the lives of others, the better positioned you will be.

Contributing is a selfless act. Certainly the rewards will not always be immediate, that is one of the reasons why people do not give. However, if you decide to dedicate your life to helping others, you will find unlimited rewards and satisfactions.

When you take care of others, others take care of you.

10. Finish what you start

It is easy to move forward in life if we commit ourselves to finish what we started. In fact, the only reason there are chaos and disorganization is that people did not commit to bringing their actions to an end. A person who finishes his things well is a champion who always wins because he is founded on integrity.

This word refers to doing what needs to be done, even if the consequences are not in your favor. In the long term you will be stronger and others will know that you are a reliable person.

Creating the life of your dreams is a process of resistance, but in your way you will find that there are many people willing to help you create your vision and work for your goals.

CHAPTER 10: *ACHIEVE SELF-DISCIPLINE AND FOCUS ON ACHIEVING YOUR GOALS*

What are the decisions that make the difference between staying stagnant and reaping success? Those that challenge you to get out of an easy and comfortable routine, to focus on achieving goals. Getting self-discipline is key to making these kinds of decisions.

There are differences between:

- Work to be happy, to grow and conform to your current situation.
- Get up earlier for physical activity and spend a sleepier hour.
- Invest time in training and spend time at leisure.
- Continue fighting to reach the goal and leave when the first obstacle arises.

Focus on getting quick rewards, on something sure, you will hardly achieve the desired goals.

Self-discipline will take you to work to achieve your goals regardless of whether you are motivated or not, to later enjoy the benefits of realizing those goals.

How to achieve self-discipline in your personal and professional life?

Self-discipline obeys purposes not impulses

To achieve self-discipline and work on your development, you must focus on objectives.

It usually happens that knowing a success story, a feat, inspires and motivates you to carry out a similar purpose. For example, participate in a pedestrian marathon and complete the 42-kilometer journey.

If this is an aspiration based on the moment, either because you have known the protagonist of the story, for the joy of success, how long will the motivation last to achieve this yearning?

Without self-discipline, motivation will decrease over the course of days.

Achieve self-discipline as an ally in the long term

Following the example of participating and completing the marathon course, it goes beyond just one impulse. As in all purposes, it is necessary to be clear about what is required to achieve it, what challenges are being assumed. In this case to prepare and obtain a physical condition necessary for athletic competition:

- Have A Training Plan And Carry It Out During Previous Months.
- Train Daily
- Train in Different Weather Conditions; Heat, Cold, High Humidity.
- Get Up Earlier Than Usual.
- Carry Out A Diet According To The Training Stage.
- The Training Progresses, the Effort Is Greater.

- The Body May Resent the training effort.

Something very important is to overcome the temptations of the short term, a routine of comfort or want immediate results.

For example, do not attend the training to attend a social meeting the day before, because it is difficult to wake up early, the training is very intense and you feel exhausted from training daily.

Maybe you think the training routine will end up getting bored and annoying you.

This posture will make you give up and you will end up abandoning. By sticking to the easy and comfortable you will not achieve great purposes.

When you focus on long-term goals, it will help you overcome these temptations. Focus on one purpose, on the benefits that the activity that you carry out will reach the goal, not just on the momentum.

By getting self-discipline, it will allow you to continue motivated in the intense conditions of your training routine.

Self-discipline supports you in the decision to continue fighting adversity instead of giving in. It helps you get on the path to the desired aspiration.

Self-discipline is to go beyond just desires. Is to work to reach goals

Work to develop self-discipline and encourage your growth. Get self-discipline for success.

Self-discipline and positive habits

How do you set priorities to achieve your purposes? At all times there are distractions that divert attention, for this it is important to protect time, respecting the space dedicated to the task to be performed.

Get self-discipline and take advantage of time in momentous goals, focus on what you should do.

Mental self-discipline for initial effort

The most expensive thing to carry out a project, a goal is just that, start. It is important to take the step from a passive state to action.

Some of the reasons that prevent the first step have to do with indecision and with the posture, perhaps I am not yet prepared. This position encourages the appearance of excuses, which continue to postpone and even cancel the project.

Apply the power of self-discipline, using a very simple technique: put yourself in front of a mirror and say to yourself just do it!

You can even repeat it mentally. This phrase will help you not only to start your projects. It will help you when you feel you are leaving your project, as well as to conclude those that are still in process.

Why everything for the last minute?

Have you had to attend a meeting where any of the presentations are obviously improvised?

What comes to light in these cases?:

- Data not updated, figures that contradict each other.
- The slides are copies of another presentation.
- The rapporteur shows no security in what he presents.

Leaving everything for the last minute, results in improvisation. Keep in mind that this way of working:

- It generates stress.
- Unnecessary mistakes are made.
- It generates a bad personal or professional image.
- They can mean loss of opportunities, be it a possible promotion, a customer who reverses the signing of a commercial agreement.

In these cases, it is necessary to get self-discipline to be a better professional, develop the positive habit of being productive and avoid delaying at the last moment to start working.

Achieving self-discipline and perseverance will allow you to take more favorable actions, such as getting ahead of work every day and not finding yourself against the wall in the time of delivery.

Getting a task on time or before, for example, a presentation will allow:

- Make a more professional presentation.
- Review figures, facts, prepare more information as support.
- Deliver quality work.
- It will allow you to focus on attendees, avoiding distractions of improvisation.
- Generate a better personal, professional image.
- You will manage to put aside stress, which is harmful to health.

Deadline

This is a positive habit, which helps prevent procasting.

When performing a task, you should avoid distractions, for example, when preparing a report, avoid those actions that divert attention, such as searching for information and suddenly you find yourself surfing the internet on issues other than the subject of your report.

This results in the consumption of available time or postponing the preparation of the report for the next day.

Focus on having a date to turn in your work, avoid being against time. Do not start at the last minute.

Keep balance

Achieving personal self-discipline has to do with achieving an optimal state to work.

Working for long hours, without rest, leads to exhaustion to lose concentration and present the risk of making mistakes, of ignoring situations that with a clear mind one does not act that way.

Alternate your work with a break to rest, to oxygenate the brain; if you are in front of your personal computer, get up and walk the other way. A very appropriate option is to perform brain gymnastics exercises.

When you carry out your activities, problems will arise and you will need to solve them. Keep the rest - work balance so that the brain can reflect in order to find the solutions sought.

Activate, apply the learning on a daily basis

The benefits of physical activity are many:

- Provides energy
- It generates a better mood.
- Improves health.
- Oxygenates the brain and improves its functioning.
- Contributes to improving physical and mental agility.

In addition to the benefits that physical activity provides to health, learning can be collected and applied daily.

Obtaining a good physical condition requires self-discipline and perseverance, to overcome obstacles, such as reluctance, the comfort of staying at home to watch television or getting up later in the morning.

Just as it happens with the exercise, in the personal and professional day to day, the reluctance, the comfort, can get to truncate the aspirations.

What can you do to get self-discipline in the activity and transform it into day-to-day learning?

Work in a team

Performing physical activity individually is fine. Design your routine and carry it out.

Joining a team of people who do physical activity will give you advantages:

- You will know routines to exercise from which you can learn and adopt.
- They will motivate you when you feel bored or think about giving up your goals.
- They will help you overcome fear, for example to participate in an athletic contest for the first time.
- You will meet people with more experience, who will advise you on how to improve your training routine, what to do to avoid injuries, will help you achieve your goals in a better time.

- You will meet more new people, with whom you will have the opportunity.
- You will know what they have done to achieve self-discipline and perseverance.

One of the best experiences of working in a team is learning best practices from others, such as overcoming fear, mutual motivation.

This means a source of inspiration and learning on how to achieve self-discipline, based on the personal history of each of your classmates.

Orient yourself to the positive

A pessimistic approach makes you focus on the difficulties, on the problems you may face and that attitude will not take you anywhere.

Orientating towards positive habits and attitudes is a decision about changing your mindset.

Focusing on the positive will help you perceive the benefits that you will get by meeting your goals.

The difference between self-discipline and procrastination, reaching your goals or forgetting them.

Learn from successful people

Even people who have achieved success have gone through moments of apathy. Self-discipline is key to overcoming it.

That the person you admire, whom you consider in an example to follow, is for you a source of motivation.

Perhaps that person has wanted to stay at home, however he decided to work to train and then lift the fruit of his effort.

On the other hand, identify those people in whom pessimism predominates since they can infect you with their attitude.

Work on getting self-discipline to dedicate yourself to your activities whether you are motivated or not. Keep in mind the fruits you will reap.

Greater effort step by step, better results

One aspect of physical activity that relates to daily life, even at the level of business has to do with working with goals and aspiring to be better.

To promote self-discipline, visualize and set goals. It is not enough to say I will go to the park to exercise. Set a goal, for example, participate in a pedestrian race.

In this way, you will find meaning every time you go to exercise, that you are training to be prepared to participate in the event.

Once you reach your goal, focus your sights on greater goals. For example, to complete a circuit of 1 kilometer, one of 3 kilometers. It will require self-discipline because it means more effort.

Be careful when investing in greater effort. Draw long-term objectives and divide them into short-term objectives, that is, move forward step by step.

It is valid that after completing a 1 kilometer circuit aspire to complete 21. But do not think about obtaining immediate results, be realistic. Let the next objective be 3 kilometers, then 5 and so on.

With this lesson you can apply self-discipline in life, self-discipline in a company. If you are a recent graduate of the university, you have obtained a job and your great desire is to become the CEO, keep in mind that you will need time to continue training, to gain experience, to develop leadership skills.

As in the example of physical activity, divide this great yearning into shorter goals and work to accomplish them.

Be organized

Keep an agenda

Work to make the time, to complete the tasks on schedule. For this, keep an agenda and organize the day, the week. Self-discipline will be of great help.

Once you have planned your activities, assign a schedule and work to accomplish them. In this way you will be more productive. Do not forget the balance, so it includes the schedule for rest periods, the schedule for meals.

Be flexible, there will be times when they appear imponderable, those are exceptions, not a reason to give up.

Focus on one task at a time

The day can contain more than one activity and its planned schedule.

Respect your agenda. Focus on the activity in turn, leave the others until their schedule. How to work only in the activity in turn? Forget the rest! You will be more productive. This is a good practice to achieve self-discipline and make it a positive habit.

Don't leave the most important task to the last

Remember, when you start the day is when you have more energy and decreases as the hours go by. Organize your agenda to focus on the most important tasks that consume you the most energy, at the beginning of the day.

Leave lower priority tasks for last.

Conclusions

One benefit of achieving self-discipline is to exercise the mind to acquire the habit of performing tasks consistently. One of the challenges in making decisions in order to start a project, is just that, start.

In this chapter, the practice of physical activity has been presented as an example to apply and achieve self-discipline. Actions such as getting up an hour earlier to perform physical activity, making a physical effort that you are not accustomed to, are surrounded by temptations and excuses to give up the attempt. It also occurs in other personal activities and even in business.

Practice and achieve self-discipline, you can carry out large projects, however, it is important to go step by step if you want to get success. A wise decision is to start with simple activities, the point is to be consistent. To establish a new habit is to learn how to be willing to carry out tasks.

10.1 Five Acts Of Self-Discipline

Self-discipline: The willpower, self-control, resolution, determination, character, driving, courage, diligence and resistance. None of these features or characteristics are produced by accident, nor do they appear by magic: They have nothing to do with luck or genetics. These values are deliberately developed and cultivated by men and women in all areas of life in order to be better. When a person possesses these characteristics, he acquires the ability to forge his destiny, through wisdom and perseverance.

Why should we follow acts of self-discipline?

Maybe we should ask ourselves: What makes us human? What distinguishes us from other living beings on the planet? The true essence of the human being seems to bring to mind endless attributes and activities, both positive and negative; for example: self-knowledge, word and symbolic cognition, agile thumbs, principles or ethics, and the ability to imagine. These are just some of the features that distinguish us from other species.

Unlike the creatures of the animal kingdom, we have the ability to choose the path we will travel in this life, since we have the self-awareness and the ability to choose between good and evil. Animals survive by their instincts, they live controlled according to their immediate desires. Human beings, however, through our training and the exercise of our free will, we can learn to control destructive and urgent impulses. We can transform behavior and negative attitudes towards creativity, positive and beneficial. Every man, woman and child enjoy this incredible ability.

Every action we take begins with an idea, a thought. We can train our mind through self-discipline to generate always positive thinking, which will always lead to positive action. Action → reaction or effect → Cause

When people are trained through self-discipline to control their thought process, as a result, their discourse will show encouragement, confidence and hope creating these feelings in other people. Because the exercise of self-discipline constantly takes maturity and wisdom, people who meet us every day begin to think that we are trustworthy and honest

If we choose a life of self-discipline, then we live in accordance with the norms, principles and ethics that put the well-being of others at the same level, not above our own! This requires training and adherence to a code of conduct and principles, regardless of whether those around us are compliant or agree with us.

If we really aspire to live in peace, then we have to learn the language of peace and speak it fluently. How can we do that? Self-discipline!

We need self-discipline if we want to help resolve conflicts in today's world, but we have to resolve our own internal conflicts first! Each individual has to achieve inner peace and cultivate it every day of their lives before we can expect to see peace in the world.

How can we follow the rules of self-discipline?

Let's look at every act of self-discipline that we have to be practicing. It would be good to examine and understand certain universal basic disciplines that apply to all people everywhere. Once we are aware of what is right and what is wrong, then through self-discipline, we can recognize the right, while avoiding the wrong!

1. Respect for the lives of people and living things

We have to respect all living beings. You will have broken this principle if:

- The victim was alive when the act of trying to kill him was performed;
- We were aware that the victim was alive;
- We intended to kill him;
- We made an effort to kill;;
- The victim died because of the effort we made to kill him.

2. Respect for the property of others

Respecting the property of others is vital to our successful survival and to be able to live in a peaceful environment. You will have violated this principle if:

- There is a person who owns the object you would take;
- We know that this person cares about this object;
- We intend to take it without your permission;
- We have put effort into trying to take it with or without your permission;
- We succeed in taking the item that was not offered to us.

3. Sexual Misconduct

In this case, we refer specifically to a dishonorable intimacy with another person: we have to learn to control our emotions, physical desires and dishonorable intimacy. It is important that when two people have a sexual relationship, it is based on mutual respect and the two people carefully and responsibly take into account the possible consequences of their actions. A person should not have physical intimacy with another if there is any risk of harmful consequences.

We have broken this principle if:

- The person we want is someone morally and ethically unacceptable (that is, married, a relative, involved in a committed relationship with another, etc.) ;;
- We intend to be intimate with that person;
- We make an effort to get intimate with that person;
- We perform physical intimacy with that person.

Bad sexual behavior can lead to:

- Cause the person to end their existing relationship with someone else
- Sexually transmitted diseases
- Unwanted pregnancy
- Emotional trauma and regret
- Reputation damage

4. False or harmful speech

In this case, we will not only include false or malicious speech, but also rude and gross speech such as gossip and "nonsense." We must make a concerted effort to speak only positive things. We will have broken this principle if:

- We say something that is not true;
- We intend not to tell the whole truth;
- We make an effort not to tell the whole truth;
- The listener does not understand things and feels offended by what we have said.

5. Using Intoxicants

Self-discipline is vital to the conscious refusing to contaminate our bodies with toxic substances, regardless of the reason, social pressure, social or cultural traditions, events or special activities of celebration. This principle has been broken if:

- The principle that we are going to have is a toxic product (for example, alcohol, tobacco, illegal and non-medicinal drugs, etc.);
- We know that the substance to be ingested is an intoxicant;
- We intend to put it, in any way, inside our body;
- We make the deliberate effort to introduce it into our body;
- Once it enters our body, it is irreversible.

If all the conditions of each discipline are not met, then we have not met them. However, if we carry out any of the conditions, we still have to be willing to accept the consequences of our actions. Accepting these consequences makes us better people. When we face the things we have done through the body, speech and mind - and not run from them - it makes us stronger and better people, with greater and genuine peaceful depth within us. Following them, we will be worthy of respect: we can walk with integrity.

CHAPTER 11: *WHAT IS PROCRASTINATE*

Procrastinating means postponing or postponing tasks, duties and responsibilities for other activities that are more rewarding but irrelevant.

Procrastinating is a way of evading, using other activities as a refuge to avoid facing a responsibility, an action or a decision that we must make.

People procrastinate in different ways, some reaching the point of becoming addicted or dependent on these other external activities, such as watching television, Internet, social networks, cell phones, playing video games, shopping or compulsive eating.

For this reason, procrastination is associated with a behavioral disorder in which the subject relates in his mind what to do with pain, change, discomfort or stress.

When procrastinating, what we do is postpone things for an indefinite and idealized future, in which we believe we will have enough time to carry out that pending issue in the way we want.

We procrastinate for various reasons: stress, anxiety, and perfectionism, fear of failure, impatience or feeling saturated with responsibilities.

We all procrastinate to some extent: the student who does his work at the last minute, the individual who leaves the delivery of forms and paperwork for the last day, the person who postpones a decision until he has no more alternatives.

However, the important thing is to reflect on what extent we are prioritizing our duties properly, taking care not to neglect the important for the urgent.

Synonyms of procrastinating are deferred, postpone, postpone or postpone.

It is necessary to know what the healthy limits to stop procrastinating are. Relaxing and stop thinking about responsibilities may be necessary but you cannot flee eternally from what everyone knows you should do.

To stop procrastinating, self-discipline must be cultivated. Self-discipline is the education of the will to do what you must do constantly. The list of chores and duties and the fulfillment of simple tasks can be of great help to those who want to stop procrastinating.

How To Stop Everything Postponing?

Put off until tomorrow what could be done right away ... When it comes to procrastinating, all the degrees are possible: from a temporary blockage for such a chore that we push back punctually, until the sustainable trend to postpone everything with very sensible material consequences. But how to understand procrastination and especially avoid giving in?

Do not do things right away, when they are painful, may seem quite understandable. But not everyone adopts this strategy, we can even say that about half of people prefer to get rid of chores immediately to have peace of mind and then devote to things more enjoyable. The others opt for the opposite solution: start with the pleasant things to finish with the most annoying ones. If you are in this situation and procrastination has become a real problem for you, let's go!

Anxiety of uncertainty

One of the main factors that drive procrastination is anxiety. As with phobias or anxiety disorders, deferring action is an equivalent of avoidance behavior, which cancels (transiently) the stress associated with it. Depending on the context, this anxiety may be related to uncertainty, lack of self-confidence, or any other fear generated by the action to be taken or its potential consequences. It can include social anxiety, for example for appointments that are rejected or for objectives that have an important collective dimension.

Uncertainty and lack of control over the situation are decisive factors. Not knowing well in advance the whole problem to be confronted, not knowing how much time it will be necessary to devote to it and especially not having previous experience of the same task and thus of its realization constitute major obstacles to the triggering action, especially when one lacks self-confidence. Thus, whenever we have the choice between an uncertain action where we risk becoming bogged down and an action that we master, we will choose the second obviously.

Want to do too well

Beyond the lack of control of a situation, a fundamental problem often explains the habits of procrastination: low self-esteem and its corollary, perfectionism. To constantly want to do things in a perfect way, to prove oneself one's own value, which one doubts in reality, quickly creates a vicious circle: setting the bar too high inevitably leads to not reaching it, which ends up altering even more. image that one has of oneself ("I never arrive at nothing", "It is the proof that I am worth nothing"...). This race to perfection prevents action, and it can even directly make procrastination: rather than confronting a possible failure, we prefer, even without really realizing it, not to try at all.

Time estimation

The question of time is central in procrastination, since we are always late. The people involved often have a problem with the estimate of the time that can take such action, with a clear tendency to underestimate the necessary time, and overestimate the time remaining before the last limit. This can be likened to an excess of optimism, or sometimes also to the politics of the ostrich: with the intuition of the delay that we begin to take, we prefer not to think about it and not to confront the reality. Thus, it is too late and we feel overwhelmed, not because the task was too difficult but because we did not spend enough time.

Another type of trap also explains the strengthening of procrastination: false emergencies. Rather than embarking on an important and late task, one prefers another, less important but more affordable (less complex, more enjoyable). This with a pretext for self-depreciation, the type: "I really have to do it now, it cannot wait. And, from false emergencies to false emergencies, the necessary things are postponed indefinitely.

Finally, the last factor of procrastination is, paradoxically, a tendency to hyperactivity. When it is disordered, with real problems of attention as in some children but also in many adults, the risk is not to be able to build an action continuously from beginning to end. Excessive distractibility leads to effectively moving from one subject to another, and thus does not perform any task completely. The people concerned are thus lost in many actions, begun but interrupted, and do not find themselves anymore. This tendency to dispersion and lack of concentration is naturally amplified by all the incentives for distraction, especially from various screens and other digital media.

Attention to good resolutions

Just as it is futile to decide to start a diet from one hour to another (it does not take very long in general ...), the great resolution "I completely stop procrastinating today" has not meaningless and is rather counterproductive. Without preparation or plan of action, you risk failing very quickly, to discourage you in guilt and not be able to tackle the problem for a long time ... It is necessary to go from an illusory logic of all or nothing to a reasoned procedure and targeted.

The preparation for change is to analyze one's own behavior, to be sure of one's motives (why should I change and what do I expect from it?), and to set goals based on a quite precise method. You probably have late tasks in different areas: work, studies, storage of clothes or books, filing of papers, payment of bills, DIY, etc. Establish priorities based on the following two parameters: the degree of urgency and utility of the task to be performed on the one hand, and the level of difficulty and difficulty on the other hand.

The preferred setting is the degree of utility and urgency, because advancing on these topics can make your life easier quickly, and most importantly will boost your motivation and self-confidence if you succeed. So choose the actions that you have been pushing for a long time, even if you do not have mandatory deadlines set by external conditions (these are often the ones you push back to infinity), and that really matters to you or your relatives.

If there are several, apply the second criterion to rank them: first those who should ask you the least effort and time, then the others.

Ten small problems are better than one big one

Another essential rule in the fight against procrastination is the segmentation of problems. Unable to complete a large task of great complexity in one go and on a short time. It is essential to break down the heaviest actions into more affordable sub-actions, taking less time and less difficulty when they are processed one after the other. For example, if your main goal is to tidy up your room or cellar, it's easy to segment this task into sub-parts: first put away a piece of furniture, then another, then some drawers, and so on. This will not allow you to ask too many questions when you are in action, since the task is well defined. And especially to get a real satisfaction every time

It is essential to introduce rewards when you achieve goals, things that you will not be allowed to do until you have completed the contract. This self-gratification may seem a little rudimentary or trivial, but it really works to maintain motivation.

A good stopwatch

If you feel your determination fragile, at least initially, I recommend the method of rounds. Just as you have cut out the task to be achieved in several slices of objectives, it is useful to cut the time in rather short periods, like the rounds of a boxing match. These periods, which may be ten minutes for example, are a good guard against the risk of distraction.

The rule to fix yourself, and to respect as strictly as possible, is to do nothing more than the task scheduled during the ten minutes of each sequence. You can give yourself a break at the end of each round by doing something else or nothing at all (rest), or choose to chain right away for another ten minutes if you feel good. But the same discipline is essential for all future sequences: do nothing more than the task and rely on objective time measurement, using the stopwatch of your smartphone for example.

The rewards you grant yourself should not risk getting you drifting too long from your main mission ... So no addict genic activity, like a game you cannot get away with! Similarly, care must be taken not to be distracted during the task by all the usual temptations, especially from your phone or computer. Be sure to turn off the devices during the important work phases, or at least turn off all notifications. Keep in mind that your concentration will be difficult to maintain if the task to be done is not very pleasant or requires an effort of reflection or attention therefore, so protect yourself against all temptations.

Goal Management and Time Management

From beginning to end, you risk being slowed or even paralyzed by your need for perfection or at least your desire to do well. We have seen that this tendency, laudable in principle, can be a real poison of action. So you have to be prepared to flush out behind any criticism of yourself, or behind any attempt to quit acting or continuing work. You will not be able to do everything perfectly, it is certain, but all that will be done will be a step towards your satisfaction. Be uncompromising with your perfectionism!

Two last tips:

1. Try to identify the times of day in which you are usually the most productive. We all have slightly different profiles: some work effectively early in the morning, others in the evening or at certain times of the day. Try to consider these particularities when planning your most energy-intensive activities.
2. Sometimes go into "emergency" mode when things are not working well enough. You have probably already noticed that your productivity is significantly increased when you absolutely must make work before a date unavoidable, or when a deadline is imposed on you for practical reasons (departure on vacation, move, visit a friend, etc..). These are moments when all our energy and especially our motivation are concentrated on a single objective, with a notion of urgency forcing a certain speed. This is why some people end up, more or less deliberately and consciously, by getting into the habit of working at the last minute to gain efficiency. But it is possible to reproduce this pressure by obligations that one imposes on oneself: to oblige oneself to finish one task absolutely before such a date considering that it predominates above all the rest. This requires a tighter time schedule than you would tend to grant spontaneously.

This strategy can bring a lot, but it is best not to abuse it because it can lead to excessive fatigue and stress. Try to alternate periods of normal organization with these intense rush beaches.

The essentials against procrastination:

- Prioritize your goals and start with the ones that matter the most while having the least difficulty.

- Segment tasks into sub-actions that are easier to do.

- Set up ten-minute sequences during which you do not have to do anything other than the scheduled task.

- Organize your activities according to the abilities you know, including the days or times when you are usually the most productive.

- Go into "emergency" mode when blockages resist, setting yourself a mandatory deadline not to exceed.

For further

"Why do today what can be postponed to tomorrow? ": A question that may have already touched your mind. If some say it lightly, lip service, others apply it literally, preferring to postpone things and thus balking at the task. What about you? Do you practice the art of postponing your obligations?

CHAPTER 12: *TIME MANAGEMENT*

Time management software forces the company to structure its business and allows it to justify the work done in relation to its customers. Businesses that sell advice or service are in the front line to use it.

What is time management? The management of time, to put it simply, is to optimize his schedule and his schedule, while the management of time (he should be appointed more precise management of the past) is a tool for measuring services performed by a service company on behalf of its clients.

In the collective unconscious, the bulk of business trade is still based on the trading of goods and merchandise. The service is unfortunately still for many associated with "wind" and if one does not reluctant to buy material objects, that one can "touch", it is more difficult to understand or measure the value of the provision. However, it is in this area that often remains the real added value of a company.

And it is in the fact of getting to precisely invoice this added value that can reside the survival of this same company. If the grocer has a scale to measure the weight and thus the selling price of his product, the service provider rarely has a measuring instrument that is precise enough to measure and thus correctly invoice his service to his customers. . A real added value for the company! This type of software also has the advantage of "forcing" the company to structure its activity and to set up a real organization of its work.

It is therefore a matter of measuring and valuing what each employee does for each client and making it "tangible" and "quantifiable". Of course, these services must be broken down by stakeholder, by the client and by type of service, which are themselves grouped by missions on behalf of the same client.

In a simplified way, it is a question of defining at first and for each collaborator or speaker of the company the cost price and the selling price. Each stakeholder has a different skill level, so a cost price and a different selling price. This selling price can also be modulated according to the complexity of the task it performs. There are also possibilities of varying these sales prices depending on the nature of the customer.

It is therefore for the company to structure its nomenclature of work in the category of "task" and "sub-task". Finally, each stakeholder bringing a certain turnover to the company by its action, one can imagine that each stakeholder is motivated according to the annual production that it brings to the company.

It is then necessary to define for each customer of the company the missions that were discussed in the initial estimate or in the "mission letter". Each mission will be the subject of a precise listing which can be broken down into tasks and sub-tasks. Each category of work may be allocated a budget in hours and "euros" which will constitute the budget estimate. The daily input downstream of the time spent by collaborator by a client, by mission ... will then make a connection between the "planned" and the "realized". In short, it's about whether each mission is profitable or not. If in a mission, one finds losing money, it is useful to have a tool allowing to measure this in a concrete way and to be able to present a precise state to the customer in order to be able to A valuable measuring instrument for your organization and your management! Without this tool, it is difficult to be able to justify your work in relation to your client. Worse, in the event of a conflict resulting in legal proceedings, the company is completely unable to present evidence to show what has actually been done for the customer if the latter finds the fees unjustified. In addition to an indispensable management tool, the monitoring of your past times is therefore a legal obligation of any serious provider. And this should, in our opinion, be a legal obligation as well as accounting. If the company works exclusively in the past (rarer) times, the daily entry details past time information, but also disbursements and travel expenses, will allow a rigorous automatic re-invoicing. The second component is the billing of its services according to a schedule provided in advance with the client. Therefore a rigorous follow-up allows an automatic invoicing of the down payments, and at the end of the year a summary invoice of its service.

The integration of these two modules allows reconciliation between the initial budgets negotiated with the customer, the actual times spent and the billing produced on the mission. As a result, we arrive at a state that accurately measures the "profitability" of each client or mission. Indeed, one can imagine that a file is globally in loss, but it would be advisable to know if all the missions of this customer are deficit or if one loses money only on some of them. This rectifies the approach or organization of the company in this type of sector.

It is easier to understand how important it is for a company to acquire this valuable measurement tool for its organization and management. This allows them to make the right decisions in a timely manner and possibly correct a deficit or non-productive approach. Without this measuring instrument, one directs at the sight and one loses necessarily in effectiveness.

If we compare the "cost" of such a product with what the company loses every year in services that it has not been able to measure and invoice correctly, we can easily imagine that the purchase of such a product is not a cost at a loss but a real productive investment generating added value and margin.

Which companies may be interested in this type of software?

All companies that sell advice or service, so "time" and want to charge the right price these benefits. Accountants, business lawyers, service companies, consultants, architects ... This software is also intended for associations, for example, benefiting from subsidies and being obliged to justify the use made of them. . This software can also be used for simple statistical purposes, for example town halls wishing to follow the type of work done by communal workers...

Standard or specific?

Past time management is a tool that brings productivity gains to the competition! However, each company, even within the same type of activity, has a particular way of working, with a specific organization.

In a competitive environment, it is precisely in this specific organization that the company can find its strengths and its profitability, in a word stand out from the competition.

12.1 The 8 Laws Of Time Management

Stop wasting your time!

Use the laws of time management and efficiency in your daily life to find full serenity in the execution of your tasks.

These laws govern our daily lives without even paying attention to them. They are nevertheless precious allies when we learn to use them.

Used in company management, the methods resulting from these laws are adaptable to any personal or professional situation.

And then, after all ... is not maternity an immense enterprise in itself?

I'm talking to you now.

1- Murphy's Law: The Law of Maximum Emotion

Nothing ever happens as planned.

Everything that is likely to go wrong, will go wrong.

Delivered to itself, things tend to go from bad to worse.

In my opinion, this is the most verifiable law in our daily maternal life.

Who has never experienced this unpleasant experience of the price of the computer that goes to -50% the day after its purchase? From the car that does not start when the alarm clock has not sounded? Toast that falls on the jam side? From the next crate that is always moving faster?

The chance is created. Opportunities appear to open minds, and boredom is predicting. As well:

- Anticipate the improbable not to be surprised
- Split big tasks so you do not forget anything
- Is it still bad? Detach and apply a plan B

You will not always avoid hazards, but your anticipation and your reactions will determine the impact they will have on you.

And it's not bad.

2- Douglas's law: You will store your space

The more space you have, the more you spread out.

If you think you are completely overwhelmed by your daily life, start with this: As cluttering your environment is an absolute priority to move towards a better-being. Just as you take care of your physical health, you take care of your organizational hygiene. It's about your moral health.

So de- clutter your environment. This law applies to all parts of your home, but also your computer, phone...

Apply the Japanese 5 S method:

- **SEIRI:** Get rid of superfluity regularly
- **SEITON:** Storing your space so that everything has a well-defined place to facilitate its use
- **SEISO:** Clean up to prevent malfunctions and secure
- **SEIKETSU:** Maintaining order
- **SHITSUKE**: Be rigorous on the execution of the 4 previous steps to enjoy the benefits of the method

It's basic, taking care of your interior, you take care of yourself. You unclutter your head by making a clean space. Visual pollution does not promote relaxation or clear ideas.

Clean up!

3- Parkinson's law or dilation of work

All work tends to expand to occupy all the time allotted to it.

Have not you ever noticed? When you know you have 1 month to finalize your tax return, what happens 9 times out of 10?

You wait until the last moment.

And this is just one example among many others...

At Google, they offer their employees at Mountain View to use 10 to 20% of their working time to carry out personal projects, with or without the company. This seems to be an interesting way to push them to meet their deadlines on the remaining 80 to 90%.

Why not adapt this strategy to your daily life? Break down your not-so-fun tasks with little "reward" moments:

First, the reward gives the feeling of the work done, and encourages action,

Then you will need to be more proactive in completing what you have before you take advantage of it.

Example:

Saturday 14h. Your bacon is at nap. You think to enjoy the afternoon to brick the bathroom floor to ceiling.

Rather than leaving you the whole afternoon, scheduled to finish at 16h. Then on this niche of 2 hours, book 20 minutes to do something for you, which makes you happy.

It's gone, tighten the buttocks, and respect the deadline.

Enjoy your reward, and enjoy the immense satisfaction you get from this challenge. It's magical.

Hey ... Bacon is waking up

4- The Law Of Pareto: 80/20

80% of the effects are the product of 20% of the causes.

This law will help you get rid of the need for perfection, and therefore the Wonder Woman Syndrome.

Focus on what is really worth it. We often brew a lot of wind to take care of useless missions to give the impression to advance, to complete our days.

Kill the perfectionist in you.

The time lost could largely be reinvested in something more important: spending time with your family, or with yourself?

You are going to unload, already. Less work to do, less stress. By applying the law of 80/20, we find confidence in its organization, in itself. We take power on his daily life, and it feels good.

5- The law of Laborit: Start with the most painful

Start with the hardest first.

Because what is done is no longer to be done. You keep the most fun for the end, and it makes your days less heavy.

In addition, we are generally more efficient at the beginning of the day. As much to take advantage of it to knock down the pans.

You do not know where to start? List your tasks on a sheet. All you have to do for the rest of the week for example.

Choose 1 task that is particularly repulsive, depressing you, choking you.

Make it on the first niche of your day. And do this day after day.

You must do it anyway. As much to evacuate quickly.

Here is a tool that particularly helped me to prioritize and organize my daily tasks, I named: the Productivity planner.

It allows you, for each new day, to define THE main task that you will perform, then the 2 minor minor tasks that you still need to do. Finally, the 2 coolest side tasks you can do once EVERYTHING is done.

6- Carlson's Law: The interruption, the worst enemy of productivity

Any interrupted work will be less effective and take longer than if done continuously.

The restart time after an interruption is always long (about 3 minutes for a task that requires reflection).

In addition, interruptions are very frequent during a day (especially for a mother). Being interrupted every 15 minutes amounts to losing 192 minutes on a day of 16h (assuming you sleep 8h if you are lucky), which makes us a little more than 3 hours of productivity in the trash .

Huge huh?

To begin, stop drowning your brains in social networks all the time. In 2017, the French spent on average of 1h20 per day. Nothing like wasting time ... unnecessarily.

If possible, group Calls, sms, and other distractions for 2 distinct ranges during the day.

Program big tasks for moments of calm. Reserve smaller ones for more hectic time slots.

Abandon the multi-tasking.

Highly valued by a performance society completely outdated, the multi-task is a toxic poison that makes you feel incapable and mediocre. One thing at a time, you finish it, and move on.

If that's not possible, set up strong daily routines at set times to go faster and stop wasting time.

You're going to find that delicious feeling of flow: If you know, that nice feeling of being thoroughly in what you're doing and finishing things.

Nothing better for self-confidence!

7- The law of Illich: To take action without more results

Beyond a certain threshold, human efficiency decreases to become negative.

A simple principle: You cannot maintain a level of concentration, and a maximum mobilization beyond 90 minutes. It works in cycles.

Also, for 90 minutes of work, whatever it is, we take a break. Even 5 minutes. Go out to get some fresh air, drink a glass of water, pick up screens, do the housework, and take a nap. There is nothing more counterproductive than spending hours and hours trying to solve a problem. It's exhausting, demoralizing, and it does not work.

If it blocks, stop what you are doing. Take back a few hours later or the next day, depending on your energy level.

Recover your energy and full concentration for a new 90-minute cycle. You will only be more efficient and available.

Aeration of the mind and moving physically allows you to re-configure your mental space. And so, solve any problem more easily and quickly.

8- The law of Swoboda-Fliess-Teltscher, typically feminine

You will respect your biological rhythms.

Listening and capitalizing on our biological rhythms allows us to make the most of our energy.

We constantly oscillate between moments of form and recovery needs. Learning to feel these moments and follow them is a good way to save and intelligently optimize your time.

Indeed, we are not all productive at the same time, with the same power.

Hormones, genetics, internal clock, hunger, sleep, season, are all parameters of influence on our energy. Some even go as far as moons.

So how to take advantage of your own pace, to optimize your time?

In practice, analyze over a few days the times of the day when you feel full of energy, and those where you can do nothing, worse: where you nose.

When you know your rhythms, move the greedy tasks into concentration or reflection in the high energy phases. Prefer to reserve the routine tasks for the hollow moments. If you want to sleep: take 15 minutes and sleep. I give you a method to practice the nap here.

Organize your schedule according to your cycles, and help yourself with the stepping stones of energy that your body dictates. Your tasks will be less painful, you will feel less tired, you will be more efficient and faster.

The time lost is forever.

Nothing is longer and nothing is shorter. Nothing is slower and nothing is faster. All men neglect him, and all regret his loss. Who am I? - Voltaire in Zadig.

Never forget it.

Nothing replaces it. Nothing buys it. Nothing is overpowering. Time is what we have most precious. We are responsible for it, and what is made of it positively or negatively affects the course of our life, and that of those we love:

- Set your priorities with Pareto.
- Clean up your mental space with Douglas.
- Prioritize the most painful first with Laborit.
- Limit interruptions with Carlson.
- Impose deadlines with Parkinson.
- Remember to stop at the right time and you treat with Illich and Swobodan.
- And finally, protect yourself from trouble with Murphy.

By applying some of these laws on a daily basis, you will quickly find the time you need to do things that really matter to you.

12.2 Indispensable Tips On Working Time Management

1. You always have time

Everything is a matter of priority. While the time is not stretchy and a day has only 24 hours, but it's up to you to manage your priorities. If you have not finished a task in time, it is because you did not consider it urgent and did not make it your priority.

2. Days fill up faster than you think

Plan only 4 to 5 hours of work a day. Other tasks will be added as the day progresses.

3. Sometimes you are productive, sometimes not

It is quite normal to be unable to work on certain days and be able to work up to 12 hours the next day. Just accept it and give yourself 100% on the days you are productive and focused. Take the opportunity to release the pressure and relax the other days.

4. Respect your time

Consider that your time is worth 1000 € per hour: respect your time and make it respected.

5. Stop being multitasking

No, being multitasking does not save you time. This is a myth of efficiency because the brain can only do one thing at a time. By working on multiple tasks at the same time, you are not focused. In addition, your brain needs a time of adaptation to move from one task to another. As a result, you're wasting time, you're just skimming over the tasks, and you're tired unnecessarily.

6. You are more efficient when you run out of time

Have you noticed that the closer you are to the deadline, the better you are?

7. Start with small tasks

Start your day with small, simple, easy tasks to motivate and get you started.

8. Do not be a perfectionist

Perfection is not necessary and can waste time. Better a good job finished the same day that a perfect job finished a week later.

9. Do not neglect your rest time

To be productive, it is essential to be rested. If you are tired, you will not perform well.

10. Working more hours does not mean being more productive

You do not have to stay at work if you're too tired or distracted to be productive. Leave at 5pm and come back the next day, rested and motivated.

11. Organize your meetings early in the day

It is usually difficult to concentrate and be effective just before going to a meeting. So it's time lost.

12. Group your meetings and communications

Organize meeting and communication ranges (email and phone) together to achieve periods of intensive work without any interruption.

13. Control your procrastination

Use the Pomodoro technique of focusing 25 minutes on a task and then taking a break of 3-5 minutes. After 4 sessions, you can take a longer break of 15-20 minutes. There is also software that prevents you from using Facebook and others for a certain period.

14. Divide an important goal into several small goals

It is much more encouraging to finish small tasks daily and see your progress towards the end goal.

15. Prioritize your tasks

All tasks are not urgent and / or important. It is important to prioritize your tasks to avoid wasting time on trivial tasks.

16. Work on important tasks early in the day

This is where you are most effective with maximum concentration and creativity. Keep activities simpler and less creative for the end of the day.

17. Learn to delegate

If any of your tasks can be done by someone else, do not hesitate to delegate.

18. Go ahead

It is important to learn from past successes and failures. However, you must focus on your current and future projects.

19. Take notes

Write down new ideas and thoughts that cross your mind during the day. This allows you to not forget them, but above all to free your mind to focus on your work. Also note any important information or use automatic reminders.

20. Take breaks

To stay creative, your brain needs rest. To be productive, it is important to make small breaks regularly. Get out there and take time to think about something other than work. Once back in your office, you will be ready to concentrate and work effectively.

To summarize

Productivity is essential in your professional life (and sometimes in your private life). Improve your productivity by following these 20 tips and become the champion of working time management!

CHAPTER 13: *CAUSES AND CONSEQUENCES OF PRODUCTIVITY GAINS?*

Productivity gains and the sharing of these gains are major economic, political and social issues. In 1930, John Maynard Keynes argued that technical progress was responsible for rising unemployment. "We are suffering from a new evil, some of whose readers may not yet know the name - technological unemployment. It refers to unemployment caused by the discovery of new processes that save labor while the discovery of new opportunities for it is a little slower. "To understand this link, I propose to study the causes, methods of calculation and consequences of productivity gains.

What are the causes of productivity gains?

Productivity gains are generated by technical progress and work organization. These innovations are transforming the means and methods of production, products, markets and structures of the economy.

The first sector of activity to benefit from productivity gains is agriculture. The progress of agricultural production tools (tractors, plows, combine harvesters, etc.) has made it possible to reduce the hours of work and the number of agricultural workers. These gains freed up the labor needed to grow the industry and market services. By making it possible to produce more with less labor and manpower, the progress of industrial production tools (digital factories, robots, etc.) has generated significant productivity gains. The introduction of the robots has made it possible to replace the specialized workers (OS) by qualified technicians responsible for the maintenance and the maintenance of the machines.

The evolution of information and communication technologies (ICT): computers, mobile phones, videoconferencing, information processing software (ERP, CAD, CAM, CGDT, etc ...) and networks information flows (semiconductors, RFID chips, Internet, etc.) have accelerated the circulation, collection and processing of information. The progress of the means of transport (car, train, plane, cargo, tanker, etc ...) and infrastructures (highway, port, airport, high-speed line, gas pipeline, etc ...) have accelerated the movement of travelers, employees, raw materials and goods at the local, national and global levels. While ICTs reduce the time and cost of information flow, modern means of transport reduce those of the transport of goods. Combining with the elimination of tariffs, which started with the GATT agreements (General Agreement on Tariffs and Trade), these cost reductions have favored international trade, the globalization of the economy and the relocation of enterprises.

Productivity gains are also due to multiple work organization methods (Taylorism, Fordism, Toyotism, Lean management, KAIZEN, project method, etc ...), which give organizational consultants the means to restructure production and services. Toyotism, which consists in producing just-in-time production and limiting inventories to zero, requires the integration and synchronization of production tools, tracking and information processing systems and logistics.

By combining, the technical progress and the organization of the work make it possible to increase the hourly productivity of the companies.

How to calculate hourly productivity?

Productivity measures the relationship between production and the number of factors (capital, labor and hours) that are implemented to achieve it. It can measure the physical productivity of labor, the productivity of capital, the productivity of labor and the hourly productivity of labor.

- *The physical productivity of labor measures the quantity produced by a unit of factor.*

For example, it is possible to calculate the output of an employee (number of pieces made by an employee during an hour of work) or a machine (number of pieces made by a machine for one hour). If 100 employees produce 10,000 pieces, labor productivity will be 10,000/100 = 100 pieces per employee. Each employee produces an average of 100 pieces.

- *The productivity of the capital factor measures the value added (VA) generated by € 1 invested.*

For example, if a capital of 10 000 € generates a VA of 100 000 €, the productivity of the capital will be 100 000/10 000 = 10 €. Each euro invested generates on average € 10 of added value.

- *Labor productivity measures the added value produced by an employee.*

For example, if 100 employees generate € 100,000 of VA, the labor productivity will be 100,000 / 100 = € 1,000 per employee. Each employee generates an average value of € 1,000.

- *Hourly labor productivity measures the VA generated by the number of hours worked.*

For example, if 5,000 hours of work generate 100,000 €, hourly labor productivity will be 100,000 / 5,000 = 20 € per hour. Each hour of work, generates on average 20 € of VA.

- *Hourly labor productivity (workforce x average working hours) measures the value added generated by the number of hours worked.*

For example, if 100 employees, who work an average of 50 hours, generate an added value of € 100,000, the hourly labor productivity will be 100,000 / (100 x 50) = € 20 per hour of work. Each hour of work of an employee generates on average 20 € of added value.

Since it measures the performance of an employee, a workshop, a company or a country, productivity is a major indicator of the economy. The graph below compares the rate of growth of hourly productivity with that of 1 hour of work from 1950 to 2013.

The consequences of productivity gains

The goal of productivity gains is essentially to lower production costs. So this will bring positive effects first for the company. Indeed, it can reduce its selling price to be more competitive and gain market share.

If this cost reduction is not reflected in prices, the company can be more profitable and its additional profits will be used to improve its capital by investing (in fixed assets or training of employees, innovation, etc.). An increase in profits also makes it possible to better compensate shareholders and attract new ones to finance investment projects.

For employees and consumers the effects are also positive. Indeed, companies can increase wages to reward the efforts of their employees or to distribute a portion of the profits earned (profit-sharing). Consumers will see prices fall which will improve their purchasing power. This is what happened on a large scale during the economic growth of the Thirty Glorious.

Productivity can also have detrimental effects, companies put a lot of pressure on their employees, replace them with machines ... To be more productive, employees can neglect the quality of their work or favor only the profitable aspect. .

This productivity cannot be easily measured for services. How to improve the efficiency of a teacher's course and how to measure his productivity? This problem arises as soon as the service is non-market.

The essential

The law of diminishing returns stipulates that the increase in the use of a factor of production leads to an increasingly smaller improvement in the quantity of the product manufactured. But this law is contradicted in the industry where returns can be increasing thanks to economies of scale and productivity gains.

This productivity measures the efficiency of the factors of production. It is obtained by improving the conditions of production and the performance of factors of production. It allows gains for businesses as well as for employees and consumers.

However, it is difficult to measure and cannot be improved in the production of non-market services.

13.1 Strategies To Increase Productivity

Better organization of your work is the best way to do more with less. Improving productivity saves you a lot of time, and therefore money, in addition to being able to do a better job.

Changing a few small habits that you have in the office can have a big impact on your project by allowing you to do the right thing in the best way. Your customers and your state of mind will thank you.

1. Clean up your workspace

An orderly workspace also allows you to have a more orderly mindset. Start by removing from your desk, or tidy up, anything that is not essential to your work. You will first avoid distractions and give yourself a chance not to get lost in your mess.

Moreover, to classify all your documents will allow you to find them more easily and thus to save time. Do not forget to add a little something nice to look at like flowers or a photo of your family: it increases productivity by 15%.

2. Stay Healthy

A healthy body is the best way to have a healthy mind. Eating well and exercising helps you to have more energy in addition to having better memory and concentration.

Do not be fooled by coffee: it gives you energy only temporarily, in addition to causing more stress and not being good for your health.

A salad, nuts and fruits are the best accompaniments during a hard day's work.

Also, avoid having dinner at your desk to give you a good time to relax without being disturbed. In terms of exercise, it may seem like a difficult task, but it actually makes you feel happier and more productive.

In addition, you will sleep better and have less chance of getting sick to get in shape at the office the next day.

3: Quit social networks

Going to a small notification, or a message on Facebook can easily end with about fifteen minutes spent watching your newsfeed. In addition, interruptions affect your concentration and cause a drop in productivity.

The best way to resist the temptation is simply not to approach it at all when you are busy working. Reserve this time lost during your break period or at a time of the day when you answer your professional emails.

Go, disable notifications! A safe tip to improve productivity!

4. Distinguish your priorities

Start with the most important tasks to be done to ensure you have the time and motivation to do it.

Decide at the beginning of your day what deserves the most attention and set aside, at least for now, projects that are not essential to your work. Feel free to say no when what you are asked is not necessary so you do not commit to doing too many things that you cannot do properly.

Channel your energy from the beginning to what is most important to do the best work possible and less stress when you run out of time at the end of the day.

When you have checked a new task from your to-do list, it will give you a good sense of accomplishment to motivate you to continue your work.

5. Do one thing at a time

Stop thinking that multitasking allows you to do more things at the same time, it just makes you take more time doing both things than if you did them separately.

Experts believe that by doing this, you lose 40% of your productivity. First, you do not do two things at the same time, but rather a several things in alternation. This means that you cannot focus fully on activity and take more time to understand where you are when you start working on a task.

In addition, too much workload is more likely to stress you. What really helps is to do several things one after the other, since it keeps you in the same state of mind. For example, try to answer your emails one after the other rather than separately during the day.

6. Impose a Time Limit

Limiting the time you invest in a certain activity allows you to set a productivity goal more clearly and avoid spending too much time performing a task. Then think about taking a few minutes to organize your work day by planning the time you expect to spend on each task.

It is also advisable to do the longest activities at the beginning of your work schedule in order to be sure of being able to execute them. This will allow you to better realize everything you have in mind by focusing more on the important tasks and less on the more futile tasks.

Seeking perfection can often be more harmful than you would have thought.

7. Take a break

There is no point stuck in a project that gets you tired and does not inspire you anymore, you will only waste time without really going forward. It is advisable to take a break before having done 90 minutes of work in order to be as efficient as possible since the productivity begins to decrease after 50 to 60 minutes of continuous work.

Studies show that taking short breaks allows you to have a consistent level of performance in addition to improving your focus, receptiveness, creativity, interpersonal skills and quality of life.

This little moment of relaxation is even more effective if you take the time to do a little exercise since you can also reduce your physical tension.

8. Create a corporate culture that ensures a pleasant working climate

I am one of those who believe that a good corporate culture increases the productivity of employees. You win, in my opinion, to establish strong values within your company. You can also develop routines with initiatives that give your employees the opportunity to excel, to create connections between them so that they can use their creativity. At my office, for example, I make sure that the people we work with are passionate about their field of activity. I make it an essential value of the company by remembering the importance of being authentic and having fun while working. When there are drops of energy, motivation or moments of fatigue, we have the reflex to invite ourselves to take a walk outside. This quickly puts us back on the peak. Sending text messages or weird e-mails also helps us get off to a good start. We also invite the tenants of our co-working space to participate in some of our activities so they can get to know each other better.

9. Communicate clearly and regularly with your employees

When you give a mandate to one of your employees, it is in your role that it is clear and well understood for you to achieve good results. The mandate must be SMART. That is specific, measurable, achievable, realistic and temporarily defined, more precisely with a schedule. Regular communication with your employees is also essential. For my part, each beginning of the week begins with a moment reserved to look at what we will work during the week and at the beginning of the day, we give ourselves a little follow-up where we went in our files. In addition, it is important to quickly share with your colleagues or collaborators your pride for the good moves they have made. It's free and a good dose of energy drives us and surrounds us.

10. Use new technologies

There are more and more collaborative tools that facilitate teamwork in business and it's a winner to use them. I think, among others, Basecamp, Google Drive that we use a lot and ever note. I also recently discovered Plan zone, an application that allows you to stay connected with your team anywhere, anytime (everyone knows in real time what to do) and do project management. The application is free for 14 days and already has more than 10,000 users. Remember that in any case, before selecting a tool, it is important that you understand your needs.

11. Train your employees

Your employees have been recruited to help grow your business, and they expect to gain experience in their field of activity as well as to excel. It is therefore in your duty to give them the opportunity to improve through internal or external training. In addition, your employee may miss the point at some point. You must remember that this happens to everyone. Rather than blame him, think of encouraging him to better understand his mistakes to prevent them from happening again.

12. Subcontract

To allow your team to focus on their strengths and specialties, it is very advantageous to outsource some mandates. With Niviti, for example, it sometimes happens to obtain mandates with peculiarities that go beyond our strengths. When this happens, we go to external collaborators to complete our mandate to meet the specific needs of our business customers. We guarantee a close follow-up overall project.

That said, my recent experiences have helped me understand that improving efficiency and productivity within a company is an ongoing process. I understand that it is a winner to stay flexible in the way of running your business. This makes it easier to adapt when unexpected events or significant changes occur.

CHAPTER 14: *AVOID DISTRACTIONS AND TAKE A MORE EFFECTIVE WAY.*

Staying focused when working in an office is a real challenge for many people. This is a daily challenge that is important to win in order to be productive. But how to proceed to achieve this? Focusing on a specific task, avoiding answering the phone, sending sms or being distracted by social networks, are all ways to get there. It is becoming more and more difficult to focus on completing tasks in this contemporary, technology-dependent world. Most of the thoughts, behaviors and devices that are useful in your daily life can become obstacles to your concentration. In order to stay focused on accomplishing your tasks, it is vital to create a work environment in which your attention will not be dispersed. Actions you can take include turning off your phones and other electronic devices, setting your schedules, and meeting a quota of work and other tasks.

14.1 Create A Distraction-Free Environment

Turn off your phone and other electronic devices: Before you start working, cleaning, writing or doing anything else, turn off your mobile phone or any other device that could be a distraction. Distraction can come from television, video games, etc. Technology is undoubtedly the biggest distraction in our modern society and being constantly disturbed by vibrations, beeps and flashes have slowed you down.

If you do not use your computer for work, shut it down or put it into hibernation.

Turn off the sound notifications of messages, emails, and tweets so you do not have to check your phone as soon as it rings.

If it is very difficult for you to concentrate, put away your devices that could become a distraction somewhere where it would be too difficult to access.

Pause your music: When you need to get to work, stay in a calm environment and free yourself from your thoughts. Indeed, your brain focuses instinctively on melodies, rhythm, and song lyrics. The music can cheer up and give the impression that time flies. However, unconsciously following the rhythm of a song in the background will reduce your ability to concentrate, whether you realize it or not.

Listen to music only after you finish a project or when you're doing simple tasks that do not require much thought.

Find a place to work better: If you are a self-employed person or do creative projects, choose a place where you can work comfortably for long periods. Your workplace may be a small corner in an office, a well-lit lanai or your favorite cafeteria. The goal is to find you in an environment that facilitates work.

Avoid environments that can affect your concentration in various ways. People tend to associate places with their usual use, so wanting to work quietly in a bedroom can make you sleep.

Arrange not to be interrupted: As much as possible, when you have big plans to achieve that requires concentration, stay away from others so you do not get distracted. Go to places where there is no risk of someone coming to interrupt you. If you work in an office, closing the door shows that you do not want to be disturbed. Although this is not possible when you share the same office with co-workers, clients, and children, you should tell them about the interactions that are allowed.

Organizing your tasks in good chronological order will allow you to do all the work without interruption.

Putting headphones on without playing music will make you feel busy, which will limit small discussions.

14.2 Ignore And Resist Distractions

Know how to recognize when you are distracted: As soon as you notice that you are viewing messages received on your phone or are viewing Internet pages that are not relevant to your work, stop and stop the distraction immediately. To be able to resist the most frequent distractions, you must be aware of the moment when you give them attention. Learn to be more attentive to resist distractions by repeating phrases like "come back here" or "it's not what I have to be doing" every time your attention drifts. Being aware of your state of mind can help you get back to reality.

Many distractions must be simply ignored. The brain is well equipped to withstand the smallest distractions and the least intrusive. However, you can strengthen your level of concentration and attention as a muscle, with a little practice.

Most people waste their time with futile activities because they fail to notice when they start to be distracted, but only realize it late, after the damage has been done.

Do not give in to the urge to procrastinate: Be disciplined when you want to start working. Procrastination is a major cause of distraction because it convinces you to do better what you need to do once you are more prepared. As soon as you realize that you will never do anything unless you start now, you will tend to postpone everything.

Procrastination is a sign of immaturity. This can lead you to shirk your responsibilities in order to feel better now.

Scientific studies have shown that people who are constantly putting things off work are less likely to succeed than those who go straight to work.

Concentrate on something: Sometimes it's important to remember to be constantly focused. Most people have never learned to really concentrate and are struggling to not disperse their attention when it comes to working. Try to end your mental distractions to accomplish your various tasks. It's not enough to know that you need to focus, but also to focus all your attention on what you're doing.

It may be helpful to remember that the best way to do everything is to focus all your attention on one task at a time. Start with one task well before moving on and so on until you reach your goals for the day.

Stay away from the source of distractions: Stay away from certain distractions that disrupt your intellectual abilities. Take with you everything you need to work or do a creative project and go to the bookstore or a quiet cafe to start working again with peace of mind. By isolating yourself, you can escape the true meaning of the term distractions that you cannot ignore. If you cannot do anything against a distraction, it is best to terminate the work and you go.

Even if you have trouble getting rid of the worst of your distractions, there are always alternatives to not thinking about it. Get out of the house without your phone, turn off the Wifi connection and close all the tabs that have nothing to do with the work you are doing.

A perfect working environment is one in which there is as little distraction as possible. The sources of entertainment involved are equipment such as mobile phones, computers, social networks, but also everything that makes you think of doing something else.

14.3 Work More Efficiently

Set a specific time to work: Choose the time of day when you are most effective and plan your schedule accordingly. If you are a morning person, wake up and get to work before slowing down and losing motivation. Night owls can divide their tasks between normal working hours and free time when everyone is in bed. Most people are only able to stay concentrated for a few hours a day. Therefore, be sure to put this time to good use.

Get in the habit of working at the same time every day and try to stick to it.

If you work at abnormal times, make others understand that they do not disturb you.

Complete the most important task first: You need to know concretely what you need to do and start with the biggest challenges. By doing this, you are sure to perform the most important tasks. You must be able to strategically prioritize so that any remaining tasks are done with the least amount of time and energy. After a while, the stress of having to perform countless tasks on hold will disappear.

When you need to outline a project, schedule meetings, and respond to correspondence, it is likely that you feel overwhelmed by the work. First, dedicate yourself to the project and then plan the rest of the day to follow up on the correspondence. This will help prevent precipitation and reduce stress.

Set a daily quota: Instead of considering the entire task, set yourself at most two goals to achieve on a daily basis. Make sure they are small and attainable. It may be hard for you to be motivated to build the fence of your garden if you only think about the time, effort and expense involved. The work will seem less daunting if you rather plan to dig the post holes one day and make up ground in the next day.

Start with small, everyday actions and increase them as you gain confidence. It is likely that you exceed your expectations by deciding to spend 10 minutes on the treadmill instead of just wanting to play sports.

It is rare to reach a goal in a short time. Stop thinking constantly that you must do everything at the same time. Setting targets in the short term means you cannot do more than you can.

Take breaks strategically: Take frequent breaks to meet your physical needs and increase your motivation. Taking small breaks for 10 to 15 minutes after each hour of work is a good guideline. This break can be used to go to the bathroom, drink a glass of water, eat a snack or rest your eyes. Do not give in to the urge to send messages to your loved ones or watch TV. The more you disperser your attention, the more difficult it will be to focus upon return to work.

The majority of people can only concentrate for at most an hour. It can be counterproductive to strive to work beyond this time because you are more likely to make mistakes or overlook important information.

Take a short walk or gentle stretching during breaks to promote blood circulation. This can contribute to your alertness and get you ready to start the job again.

Get enough rest: Make the effort to have a full night's sleep. The amount of sleep needed varies from one individual to another, but the average is six hours to be in top form. When you rest, your ability to think and work improves. Sleep relaxes the brain that has been obsessed with productivity all day and it saves you from having to think about what you will do the next day.

Turn off all your electronic devices at least an hour before going to bed. They may keep you awake!

If you are very busy, make up for lack of sleep by making short naps throughout the day.

Finally

Keeping an agenda or diary is a good way to plan your goals in the short term and assess the best moments for your productivity.

Do you impose deadlines? You can say this: "I have to finish this project by the end of the weekend. The pressure of being forced to meet an impending deadline helps many people to take action to achieve their goals.

Eat all day long. Maintaining your blood glucose level makes you more energized, improves your organizational abilities, attention to detail, and gives you the energy you need to complete your tasks. Prepare a healthy breakfast and eat something every few hours even if it's just a small snack.

Be able to rearrange your priorities as you accumulate work.

Think of ways to please yourself when you reach a goal or finalize an important project.

Finally, remember that it is your level of concentration that exposes you more or less to the sources of distraction.

You will always be distracted by something. If you cannot learn to ignore natural distractions, you will never be able to work as much as you should.

Some people are not so free to turn off their electronics. If your charges require that you use your mobile phone, tablet or computer often, you must be strict about the productive use of these devices.

CPSIA information can be obtained
at www.ICGtesting.com
Printed in the USA
LVHW060543190521
687790LV00013B/716

9 781667 112312